The Immigrant Kitchen

The Immigrant Kitchen

Food, Ethnicity, and Diaspora

Vivian Nun Halloran

The Ohio State University Press
Columbus

Copyright © 2016 by The Ohio State University.
All rights reserved.

Library of Congress Cataloging-in-Publication Data
Names: Halloran, Vivian Nun, 1971– author.
Title: The immigrant kitchen : food, ethnicity, and diaspora / Vivian Nun Halloran.
Description: Columbus : The Ohio State University Press, [2016] | "2016" | Includes bibliographical references and index.
Identifiers: LCCN 2015039567 | ISBN 9780814213001 (cloth ; alk. paper)
Subjects: LCSH: Food habits—United States. | Food in literature. | Immigrants—Cultural assimilation—United States. | Immigrants—United States—Anecdotes.
Classification: LCC GT2853.U5 H35 2016 | DDC 394.1/20973—dc23
LC record available at http://lccn.loc.gov/2015039567

Cover design by Janna Thompson-Chordas
Text design by Juliet Williams
Type set in Palatino
Printed by Thomson-Shore, Inc.

♾ The paper used in this publication meets the minimum requirements of the American National Standard for Information Sciences—Permanence of Paper for Printed Library Materials. ANSI Z39.48-1992.

9 8 7 6 5 4 3 2 1

For my three half-immigrants:
Maria Elena, Thalia, and Billy Carlos Halloran

Contents

	Acknowledgments	ix
Introduction	Food in the Immigrant's Domestic Life	1
Chapter 1	From Academic Sojourners to Settler Migrants: "Scholarship Boy" and Girls in the Kitchen	21
Chapter 2	Eating in Public as Performance of Assimilation, Diaspora, or Ethnic Belonging	41
Chapter 3	Mapping the New South(west)ern Home	64
Chapter 4	Expats in Love: Recipes for Belonging Abroad	88
Chapter 5	Diasporic Inventions: Reclaiming Family Culinary Traditions	109
Conclusion	Talking Turkey: The Thanksgiving Holiday as the Measure of Assimilation	128
	Works Cited	143
	Index	149

Acknowledgments

This book grew out of my experiences moving to the United States from Puerto Rico, and trying to recapture the aromas and flavors of the kitchens of our family matriarchs: my maternal grandmother, Tata, and my mother's godmother, Leíto. Stumbling cross Austin Clarke's *Pig Tails 'n Breadfruit* many years later, while on a conference trip to Barbados, opened my eyes to the strong connection one can feel toward one's own national and ancestral history through food. It also gave me a more diasporic perspective on Afro-Caribbean foodways that both acknowledged and challenged the discourses with which I was familiar, which lauded the primacy of soul food as a culinary manifestation of pan-Africanism. By reading this memoir, I discovered the work of this great craftsman whose fiction I have enjoyed reading and teaching for the past ten years. To Mr. Clarke, then, I extend my thanks, for being such an inspiration.

I would also like to thank the writers whose work I examine in these pages. Sharing personal details of one's life is never easy, and they have all done so with grace, wit, style, and incredible generosity. I follow several of them on Twitter, and thus, I feel privileged to get ongoing glimpses into their lives and the central role that food continues to play within them as a means of building community, offering hospitality, and sharing wisdom. Reading your works taught me a lot about how to communicate my own experience of immigration to my American-born children, and how to question my own assumptions about how I can best pass on my cultural, national, and gastronomic heritage to them as their legacy. Considering this archive as a whole made me aware of how eloquently one can describe one's appetites and the struggle to fully satisfy them. I have amassed a library of primary sources many times larger than the selection discussed here, and I look forward to continuing my reading in this area for the rest of my life.

In some way or another, I have been working on becoming a literary food studies scholar since I arrived at Indiana University (IU), Bloomington in 2002. I wish to thank the hundreds of students who have enrolled in my food classes offered through the Departments of Comparative Literature (Food in Popular Culture, Book Bites), American Studies (American Appetites, What is America?: From Acorns to Zombies), and English (Research in Colonial and Postcolonial Studies); the College of Arts and Sciences (Global Appetites); the Hutton Honors College (Food Literature); and the Intensive Freshman Seminars (American Appetites, Zombies). Not only have my students patiently read food memoirs and novels about food and written thoughtful analytical essays about them, but they have also watched TED talks on sustainable urban agriculture and food waste, worked at the IU campus gardens, posted Yelp! reviews of local restaurants, deconstructed Super Bowl food ads, listened to food-themed songs, heard my play-by-play about the previous night's episode of *Top Chef*, and learned to tweet and create fun and informative projects using Storify, Tumblr, and Pinterest, among other platforms. Most admirably, my students have also eaten food I've cooked by following recipes in the books discussed here and others through the years. For that, I thank them most sincerely.

My students and I have all benefitted from the generosity and expertise of Carrie Schwier from the IU Archives, who shared her boxes of primary source documents about the madrigal dinners held for years at the University Club at the Indiana University Memorial Union. Carrie patiently answered my questions and those of the students, who followed up on their visit and spent time looking through primary sources themselves. At the Mathers Museum of World Cultures, Sarah Hatcher has led countless tours of my food students on tours of the permanent collections, and has also taken my honors students and me downstairs to the vaults on behind-the-scenes tours of the museum's holdings. She has been more than patient with me as I incessantly ask about the provenance of this or that object, and run crazy ideas by her about how best to incorporate museum holdings into my assignment design so as to extend opportunities for student learning from the collections beyond the actual visit.

At the Lilly Library, I have worked with Becky Cape, now retired, former head of reference and public services, and Rebecca Baumann, education and outreach librarian. Both Becky and Rebecca have always patiently put together engaging selections from the cookbook collection at the Lilly for my students to look through and get excited about. When we introduced Twitter to the visits, we ended up with phenomenal results, including accounts of students who prepared the dishes whose recipes they photographed. This was an experience I cannot wait to try again. Finally, at the IU Art Museum, I have to thank Nan Brewer, Lucienne M. Glaubinger curator of works on paper, for her boundless enthusiasm for this topic, and her willingness to put together behind-the-scenes tours for my food students so they can get up close and personal with works on paper ranging from Breughel to Warhol, and everything in between. She has also introduced me to the work of many artists whose work depicts food in unexpected ways, from hyperreal diner paintings to prints made with comestibles like coffee grounds or blueberries; she has found an immense archive to share with me. It has been an education, and I look forward to learning more.

My colleagues in the Food Studies faculty group and the Sawyer Seminar on Food Sustainability have been extremely supportive; among them I wish to thank Professors Rick Wilk (Anthropology), Dan Knudsen (Geography), Carl Ipsen (History), and Peter Todd (Cognitive Sciences) for their mentoring and willingness to listen to my literary perspective on all things food-related. Being part of the planning committee for the 2014 Food Themester in the College of Arts and Sciences, "Eat, Drink, Think," has also proved to be another source of inspiration. I also want to thank Professors Whitney Schlegel (Biology) and Andrea Wiley (Anthropology) for welcoming me into the Human Biology faculty during each of their terms as director of the program. Thanks to Human Biology, I have gotten up close and personal with many a pig's digestive tract, and as a result I have a fuller appreciation for tripe and chitterlings than I ever did before.

I want to thank Purnima Bose (English and International Studies) for the many delicious home-cooked meals to which she has invited me, as well as for her encouragement during our weekly writing boot camp sessions. I am in awe of the depth of her knowledge and also afraid to disappoint her, so that keeps me honest and working rather than chit-chatting. I also want to extend my family's thanks to Kip and Whitney Schlegel, who have warmly welcomed us to their farm to celebrate Thanksgiving for almost a decade. This has become a beloved tradition, one we look forward to all year, and their warm hospitality and delicious food always make us feel at home.

Paula Cotner and Carol Glaze have shared their home-cooking wisdom throughout the years. Whether it's listening to Paula detail the process her family goes through to make bushels of apples from her uncle's orchard into apple butter, or Carol talking about cooking the game her husband brings home, I have learned a lot about American food that I never would have otherwise. I'm still waiting to try Carol's fried squirrel or some of Paula's morels, but I'm sure we'll get around to it someday.

David Halloran has patiently lived with this book for many years. He has happily served as a taste tester whenever I decide to try out recipes from these memoirs, he has listened to me work out the ideas for each of these chapters as they have clarified and taken shape, and he has put up with me as I watch cooking shows, food documentaries, and anything Anthony Bourdain broadcasts into the world, all in the name of "research." He has also read multiple drafts of this manuscript and sat in the audience at the many conferences where I have presented bits and pieces of this work in process. For that, and for not divorcing me when I served him purple chicken soup as a newlywed two decades ago (who knew red cabbage would turn soup stock purple?), I will be eternally grateful.

Introduction

Food in the Immigrant's Domestic Life

One crisp, November day in 1988, just over a year after my family and I had moved from Puerto Rico to Aurora, Colorado, I opened the door to go get the newspaper but instead found a surprise waiting for us on the doorstep: a basket filled with a frozen turkey, a can of cranberry sauce, a box of stuffing, and another box of instant mashed potatoes. There may even have been a few sweet potatoes and some marshmallows as well. Nestled among the food items was an unsigned card wishing our family a happy Thanksgiving. I called my mother to come inspect this unexpected bounty. She went out onto the driveway and looked around for any trace of our unseen benefactors, to no avail. Our first reaction was mixed: on the one hand, we were touched that others had reached out to us with such a welcoming gesture, while on the other hand, we felt embarrassed because we could afford to buy our own holiday meal, though turkey is not necessarily what would have graced our table since pork was more to our taste. We hoped that we had not deprived a poorer family from receiving food that they needed. Since there was no way to contact whoever had given us the fixings for the Thanksgiving meal, we decided to accept the gift in the spirit in which it was given, as a sign of welcome extended by our neighbors to a family of recent immigrants.[1]

---

1. Since 1917, all Puerto Ricans have had automatic U.S. citizenship at birth, thanks to the Jones Act, signed into law by President Woodrow Wilson. This means

My mother thawed the turkey, and a day or so later, we had our feast. We said grace over the meal and felt truly grateful that "the Americans" had welcomed us among them. Receiving such a gift made me believe, for the first time, that the United States could be my home, not just the place I lived.

Nowadays, the only time I pause to think about my family's move to the United States is when my oldest daughter, Maria Elena, teases me about my Spanish accent, which becomes more pronounced when I am angry or surprised. My usual response to her playful banter is to scold: "Don't make fun of your mother; she's an immigrant!" This type of intergenerational labeling has become a family ritual and a joke that defuses tensions; however, while this performance explicitly marks my own place within the family and the wider community, Maria Elena's situation remains undefined. If one of your parents is an immigrant, what does that make you? Maria Elena answered that question for herself soon after we bought her first cell phone. She proudly added her number to my contact list, but it was not until the first time I tried calling her that I noticed that the child had added "half-immigrant" as a self-descriptor just below her name. Apparently, all of the joking references to my immigrant experience had a direct influence on how my oldest daughter constructed her identity as the child of a Puerto Rican woman and a Midwestern American man. Partly, this was her way of extending our joking banter into the realm of our future phone conversations (which turned out to be carried out primarily through texting), but her word choice was also the result of her upbringing: Maria Elena is the only one of our three kids to have a Spanish name, and she took to learning my native language with a passion.

She constructs her identity as American with a difference, and yet the one area in which this otherwise adaptable young woman has adamantly refused to perform her half-immigrant identity is in the context of food. Whereas her younger sister, Thalia, loves eating the Puerto Rican national dish of rice and beans, followed by some guava paste for dessert, Maria Elena prefers Mexican-inspired burrito bowls without any type of beans at

---

that they can travel back and forth between the island and the States without need of either a passport or a resident visa. I nonetheless describe my family's experience of moving permanently to the United States from Puerto Rico as "immigration" rather than mere "relocation" because of the profound culture shock we experienced. Linguistic, cultural, and religious differences are so pronounced between the Caribbean island and the U.S. mainland that the process of acculturation and adjustment Puerto Ricans go through is similar to that of others who have had to renounce their citizenship and claim of belonging to their birthplace in order to make a new life in the United States. We simply don't have to deal with the paper chase and waiting period associated with the process of naturalization that others do.

all. Their brother, Billy, lives on chicken nuggets and dumplings with soy sauce. My parents, who have retired to Missouri, consider my Irish American husband to be an "honorary Puerto Rican" since he enjoys eating my mother's *lechón* (roasted pork leg) and *amarillos* (fried sweet plantains), as well as the *asopao* (Puerto Rican chicken and rice stew) I make when it gets cold outside. I used to prepare Puerto Rican food more often when the kids were younger and we lived in Los Angeles, but moving to a college town in the Midwest has sparked my interest in lighter fare. These days, I like exploring locally grown fruits and vegetables and trying out new recipes I find through my Twitter feed. Though mealtimes at our house are often made challenging by our clashing food preferences, all five of us like to cook, eat, and discuss food and recipes with one another.

My daughter's claim of being a "half-immigrant" makes me wonder to what degree I still continue to feel particularly marked by my arrival in this country.[2] How much have I changed since that first Thanksgiving parcel arrived at my parents' doorstep? Can I remember the "foreign" taste of that first American turkey? The novelty of cranberries? The Thanksgiving meal is quintessentially a celebration of putting down roots and making it past the first obstacles to settle in for the long haul. Is this how the meal worked for my family? For other, more recent, immigrants? In sharing this anecdote with my own family as I prepare foods that have such a clear cultural resonance for me, what am I telling my children about themselves? What have they taken away from our table as they go out into the world? These questions inspired me during the writing of this book. After all, my sense is that the longer I have lived in the United States, the less my cooking repertoire is defined primarily by my Puerto Rican upbringing, and the more it reflects the influences of my academic research, adventurous restaurant eating, and eagerness to try new ingredients from my local supermarket. Yet, when I occasionally feel homesick, nothing brings me as much comfort as the enticing aromas of a plate of homemade rice and beans.

---

2. My family's move to the United States when I was a teenager was prompted by a desire to have access to better medical care than was available in Puerto Rico, and thus the trauma surrounding our move and acculturation had as much to do with illness in the family as it did with the shock of getting used to people constantly inquiring where we were "really from" when they heard us speaking Spanish in public. The anxiety I have apparently conveyed to my daughter about the difficulty of assimilation, thus, is focused linguistically: do I "sound" American, or will my usually dormant accent "give me away" as an outsider in an unguarded moment? As someone who has learned to speak Spanish, Maria Elena identifies as a "half-immigrant" because she simultaneously knows she *is* an insider in American society, whereas I have only learned to function *like* one.

The primary argument *The Immigrant Kitchen* advances is that immigrant culinary memoirs with recipes render the topic of immigration palatable to a wide readership; the recipes offer an additional avenue of explanation and exploration for an audience invited to dine as members of this imagined community. By offering a glimpse into the domestic lives of "exemplary" immigrants through discussions of homemade food, these nonfiction texts help demystify for a mass audience the related processes of immigration, assimilation, acculturation, and even expatriation. I put the adjective "exemplary" in quotations because I want to stress that what makes these memoirs less contentious than the contemporary political discourse surrounding immigration reform is the implied assurance they supply that the immigrants in question, whether the writers themselves or else their parents or grandparents, followed the rules and arrived in this country with the "proper" documentation. The immigrant food memoir with recipes is necessarily a product of legal immigration precisely because the texts and the recipes included within them are just another way these writers *document* their journeys and arrival into this country. All the writers featured here have the luxury of mapping their differences from mainstream society rather than having to blend in or hide in plain sight as undocumented migrants do to avoid deportation. Ironically, few of these memoirs spend much time discussing the actual immigration process, preferring to focus on what it means to live as naturalized citizens of the United States or their descendants, the half-immigrants among whom my daughter counts herself.[3]

As both a literary genre-study and a food-inflected work of American studies scholarship, *The Immigrant Kitchen* analyzes texts published by accomplished writers who are themselves immigrants or the children and/or grandchildren of immigrants, such as novelists Austin Clarke, Diana Abu-Jaber, and Denise Chávez; dramatist Eduardo Machado; and renowned cookbook authors Madhur Jaffrey and Colette Rossant, among others. I put their memoirs with recipes in conversation with similar works by African American writers like the late Maya Angelou and playwright/poet Ntozake Shange, whose families also faced internal displacement during the decades of the Great Migration, when people left the South in search of better economic opportunities in other regions of the United States. As a group, these

---

3. The current political debate regarding immigration reform demonizes the "undocumented" immigrant or "illegal alien," two categories that describe those subjects who either overstay their legal visas or else who cross borders without the benefit of official sanction in order to seek economic opportunity in the United States through their own initiative. In discussing these marginal figures, political figures and commentators emphasize the criminal or unlawful aspects of their presence in the country.

public figures and memoirists recall their respective childhoods as a series of memorable meals and through this trope examine the complex set of interrelationships that contribute to identity formation on the basis of class, race, nation, ethnicity, and/or diasporic membership status. These writers, some of whom are immigrants themselves, and the vast majority of whom I consider, after my daughter, to be half-immigrants, discuss the emotional toll that listening to their parents' sometimes-harrowing stories of escaping war, experiencing discrimination, or simply feeling culture shock and disorientation took upon their own view of themselves as Americans marked by their elders' experience of immigration.

By narrowing the scope of inquiry to focus on the work of established writers addressing their existing readership, this study analyzes the allure of the legal immigrant's textual performance of culinary domesticity for an eager audience of literary-minded "foodies" who value the personal connections the writers feel toward the dishes they recall so fondly.[4] The goal of *The Immigrant Kitchen*, then, is to expand the working definitions of what constitutes life and food writing beyond the cookbook or biography of an eating life. The book also aims to give the hybrid subgenre of the food memoir with recipes its due as a complex and engaging mass media product simultaneously catering to multiple reading constituencies and doing different types of cultural work: entertaining readers with personal anecdotes and recollections; teaching new skills through the recipes; sharing insight into different cultural mores through its ethnographic and reportorial discussions of life in other countries; and, finally, attesting to the impact that an individual's legal immigration into the United States continues to have down through the generations of his or her American-born families. Thus, the critical framework I employ in my readings of these texts is likewise interdisciplinary so as to properly evaluate the function of this literary subgenre. Among the interpretive strategies I pursue are a postcolonial reading of the United States as an imposing, independent nation-state profoundly interconnected to the countries that comprise the Commonwealth of Nations through their shared legacy of British imperialism; a transnational analysis of the diasporic circuits immigrant families traverse to maintain filial ties; a comparative ethnic remapping of the cultural geography of the South into the New South based on border theory and recent immigration

---

4. Bittman 2014. I agree with Mark Bittman that the word "foodie" serves as a problematic shorthand for food aficionados or fans. My use of the term in this context reflects his expanded definition to encompass people whose enthusiasm for food writing, good food, and food entertainment are all part of their larger political commitment to food security and social justice.

and ethnic resettlement patterns; a feminist critique of the fiscal burdens and professional limitations expatriation places on women who accompany their male partners overseas; and a cultural studies analysis of the use value of reclaimed or invented culinary traditions in the context of the familial duty to reconnect with a previously unappreciated cultural heritage. I conclude by coming full circle and analyzing Thanksgiving-themed films about immigrants and how they find their place within this American national food holiday, much as my family did when we discovered the basket of goodies on the doorstep.

Immigration, Naturalization, and the "Crypto-Foreigner"

By expanding the definition of what constitutes American-ness to account for racial, linguistic, religious, and gastronomic difference as well as overlapping memberships in multiple imagined communities—both domestic and diasporic—the memoirs with recipes examined here do not merely proclaim diversity, but instead make it possible for readers to access it in tangible ways. Historian Hasia R. Diner contends that the United States became a destination of choice for immigrants from around the world because of its promise of an abundant food supply. In *Hungering for America*, she argues that this association continues unabated: "The linkage between food and migration remains valid at the end of the twentieth century, in terms not so different from those recorded for eras long past" (Diner 2001, 10). I suggest that the proliferation of the immigrant-memoir-with-recipes genre since the turn of the twenty-first century proves this connection remains unbroken. In the foreword to her memoir, *The Language of Baklava* (2005), Arab American novelist Diana Abu-Jaber comments on the inherent appeal to American readers of stories like that of her family:

> I believe the immigrant's story is compelling to us because it is so consciously undertaken. The immigrant compresses time and space—starting out in one country and then very deliberately starting again, a little later, in another. It's a sort of fantasy—to have the chance to re-create yourself. But it's also a nightmare, because so much is lost. (1)

Throughout *The Language of Baklava,* Diana Abu-Jaber repeatedly describes her father, who goes by the nicknames "Bud" and "Gus," as an immigrant torn between the hopefulness of those who choose to start life over in a new country and the intense nostalgia that prompts him to return to his homeland periodically to check if it still has a strong enough hold on his heart to compel him to stay. The loss to which Abu-Jaber alludes in this passage has to do with matters beyond time and space—in refashioning a new self, the immigrant feels the assimilationist pressure to shed those aspects of his or her personality and way of being that do not quite accord with the standards of mainstream culture in the adopted homeland. The re-creation Abu-Jaber describes takes place both psychologically, as the immigrant imagines a new way of being now that he or she inhabits a different geopolitical space, and legally, through the process of naturalization, which grants new citizens entry into the nation as an abstract legal entity, what Benedict Anderson has called "an imagined political community—imagined as both inherently limited and sovereign" (Anderson 2006, 6).

In practice, their native-born compatriots often fail to recognize some immigrants' shared insider status as fellow denizens of the polity. No matter how American they may feel, some naturalized citizens and their descendants find themselves marked as perennial outsiders, or what I call, following Linda Hutcheon, "crypto-foreigners" (Hutcheon 1998), due to their accent, name, skin color, or style of dress. *The Immigrant Kitchen* contends that the popular literary genre of food memoirs with recipes questions both what it means to be accepted as American by one's compatriots, as well as what makes up an "all-American meal." Cooking and eating are two related activities that allow immigrants and their families to embody and perform their sense of national and/or cultural belonging both privately and publicly, thus concretely addressing the sense of emotional displacement occasioned by immigrants' decision to lay claim to a new homeland.

Both immigrants and their families find a healthy outlet for the trauma of immigration in writing about the relationship between the choices they make about what to eat or cook, and their sense of claiming an American national identity while still maintaining ties of kinship to, and appreciation of, the cultural heritage of their ancestral homeland. Maria Elena's notion of the "half-immigrant" is a very good encapsulation of Marianne Hirsch's discussions of "postmemory" as an intergenerational experience of trauma, "a *structure* of inter- and transgenerational return of traumatic knowledge and embodied experience. It is a *consequence* of traumatic recall but (unlike post-traumatic stress disorder) at a generational remove" (Hirsch 2012, 6; emphasis original). Though Hirsch's trauma theory work on postmemory as both an affective category and a way of knowing is grounded in a larger discussion of the Holocaust and its aftermath, I apply her framework in this project within the specific context of immigration and assimilation to the United

States by analyzing inter- and transgenerational debates about the meaning of the past in these memoirs with recipes. Though the focus of these nonfiction narratives is ostensibly on discussions of food, their domestic contexts and references to extended family overseas illustrate for U.S.-born readers how the meals an immigrant or half-immigrant chooses to eat or disavow in public represent the contrary impulses of assimilating to the adopted country and preserving their cultural heritage.

Through their confessional tone, first-person essays featured in blogs or news websites and the prefaces of many a cookbook or individual recipe all publicly shed light on the most private aspects of the lives of fellow citizens whose customs and traditions mark them as "not quite" like the dominant society. Readers and fans of this type of "relatable" food writing learn about diversity vicariously, without the awkward risk of being perceived as either racist or insensitive for their curiosity about different cultures' customs and lifestyles. Because of its greater length and complexity, the immigrant-memoir-with-recipes genre reminds U.S.-born readers that "every American that ever lived, with the exception of one group, was either an immigrant himself, or the descendant of immigrants," as President John F. Kennedy so eloquently put it in *A Nation of Immigrants* (2008, 2). Through this careful formulation, Kennedy admits that the European model of settler colonialism in this new land came at the expense of the Native people's autonomy. Because I share this conviction that immigration has profoundly shaped the American national character in the twentieth and twenty-first centuries, my readings of selected food memoirs with recipes written by immigrants and/or their descendants acknowledge that even the major changes in U.S. immigration policy that facilitated these groups' entry into the United States failed to ameliorate mainstream society's tendency toward nativism and xenophobia. Every one of the featured writers carefully explains how he or she has constructed a personal subject position vis-à-vis the United States through the lens of ethnicity, race, national background, membership in a diasporic or exilic community, and/or linguistic ability.

Immigration Legislation

Three key immigration reforms passed after the end of World War II made it possible for these memoirists and/or their families to be granted entry into the United States. The first was the passage of the McCarran-Walter Act in 1952, which eliminated the racial restrictions imposed by earlier immigration legislation and maintained a quota system based on national origin but made allowances for people seeking refugee status. This piece of legislation made possible the immigration journeys of three of the families discussed in this book—Linda Furiya's, Diana Abu-Jaber's, and Leslie Li's. Linda Furiya's father benefitted from the repeal of anti-Japanese immigration restrictions enacted by the passage of the immigration act. Though he was born in the United States, himself the child of Japanese immigrants, his father sent the boy to be raised by relatives in Japan after the death of his mother. This meant that he was drafted into the Imperial army during World War II, and was subsequently stripped of his American citizenship. While Mr. Furiya eventually had his citizenship restored, his Japanese wife's immigration was made possible by the policies put in place by this act. For his part, Gus Abu-Jaber came to the United States from Jordan as part of the second wave of Arab immigrants who arrived after the end of World War II. His Muslim faith made him ineligible to immigrate prior to the passage of this act, though as someone who had served in the Jordanian Air Force, Gus was probably considered a skilled immigrant as defined by the terms of the act. Finally, after China fell under Communist control, Leslie Li's grandmother, the first wife of the acting president of the Chinese Republic, Li Zongren, availed herself of the refugee provisions of the same act in order to be granted entry into the United States. Unlike her former husband and his second wife, who were swiftly granted political asylum, Leslie's beloved Nai-nai had to wait eight years in a refugee camp in Cuba before being reunited with her family.

The second significant immigration reform was the passage of the 1965 Hart-Cellar Act, a revision of the McCarran-Walter Act. It replaced the nation-of-origin system with a hemispheric quota system that also prioritized family reunification and the immigration of people with skills in high demand. The third reform that directly impacts the groups discussed in this book was the Cuban Refugee Adjustment Act of 1966, which allowed any Cuban national who had resided in the United States for a year to apply for permanent residency. This act was later revised and resulted in the so-called "wet foot, dry foot" policy, now in place, which allows Cuban refugees who reach the United States to seek political refugee status, whereas those apprehended at sea are returned to the island.[5] As a Cuban exile, Mary Urrutia Randelman, as well as political refugees Viviana Carballo and Eduardo

---

5. During the Clinton presidency, this law was adjusted to deal with an increasing number of Cubans arriving on American shores after traveling in makeshift boats. What has come to be known as the "wet foot, dry foot" policy distinguishes those would-be migrants who are intercepted while still at sea ("wet foot"); they are returned to Cuba unless they seek refugee status as victims of state persecution. Those who arrive

Machado, are all covered by these immigration policies. Of the three writers, only Machado has returned to Cuba under the special exemptions to the travel ban to the island that began during the 1990s.

Together, these legislative initiatives had the combined effect of facilitating immigration from East and South Asia, the Middle East, and the Caribbean and Latin America. These new immigrants brought with them distinctive foodways that slowly became incorporated into the national palate, spicing up regional offerings and paving the way for the global food landscape proliferating in our restaurants, farmers' markets, and supermarket shelves today, as food historian Donna R. Gabaccia recounts in *We Are What We Eat*, her landmark study of immigration's impact upon American foodways. Even in this cosmopolitan foodscape, immigrants and their families may choose either to maintain their identification with the culture of their home country and ethnic heritage or to assimilate fully into mainstream culture through the mere act of partaking of popular cuisine.

Food studies scholar Anita Mannur advances the concept of "culinary citizenship" to explain the complex ways through which South Asian diasporic subjects "articulate national belonging through food" (Mannur 2009, 20). Situated at the intersections between Asian American and diaspora studies, Mannur's work evaluates a broad archive of South Asian culinary texts (cookbooks, novels, memoirs, and popular film), which together explore the limits and the possibilities of the transnational turn in ethnic studies by promoting "an alternative methodology for reading the South Asian diaspora, one that is cognizant of the dynamic interchange between the United States and other diasporic nodes" (9). This approach takes into account how class, gender, and sexuality affect the way South Asians discuss their experience of preparing and consuming food as manifestations of their ethnic and/or diasporic lives. Inspired both by Mannur's example as well as the broader range of ethnic, diasporic, and transnational backgrounds Gabaccia discusses, *The Immigrant Kitchen* engages in a different type of cultural analysis than theirs; this book's focus is on the memoir with recipes as a distinct literary genre and argues that these texts' celebration of homemade food facilitates a frank and open public discussion of the sacrifices people find worth making in order to reap the rewards of American citizenship. The wide-ranging group of writers and home cooks discussed in these pages have explored, interrogated, and redefined the category

---

upon American shores are processed and qualify for permanent residency in the United States after a year, as stipulated by the 1966 act.

of "American" from the inside out, bringing their particular immigrant-inflected perspective to their increasingly multicultural homeland.

Genre

I have used the utilitarian term "memoir with recipes" throughout this study to refer to nonfiction texts that spend as much time discussing the consumption of specific meals in familial contexts as they do recalling the art and labor that goes into putting such nourishment together. Various scholars and writers have suggested other names for food-centered narratives, but their very capaciousness makes them less than useful as tools for meaningful literary analysis. Literary critic Anne E. Goldman suggests "culinary autobiography" (Goldman 1996, 3) as an umbrella term for nonfiction books that combine personal recollections and discussions of food in *Take My Word: Autobiographical Innovations of Ethnic American Working Women*. I find Goldman's juxtaposition of the terms "culinary" and "autobiography" somewhat confusing since none of the writers she discusses either share culinary training or detail their development of a marked gastronomic sensibility in the same way, but instead, discuss both food and personal anecdotes within one text. For their part, life-writing scholars Sidonie Smith and Julia Watson advance Rosalia Gaena's term "gastrography" (Smith and Watson 2010, 148) in their book, *Reading Autobiography*, to describe what they otherwise call the "food memoir," and they apply it liberally to any work of nonfiction that makes explicit references to food and/or cooking. However, Smith and Watson warn that "the rise of gastrography may announce a radically personal form of memoir, in which 'you are what you eat,' with its provocative suggestion that the subjectivity of another can be 'cooked up,' reproduced, and tasted" (150). While I find this suggestion of the potential for textual cannibalism amusing, I have not adopted Gaena's term because it does not differ in any significant way from Goldman's concept. The last label I considered was Christine Muhlke's "foodoir," a term she coined in a book review for the *New York Times* magazine. As the then-editor of the magazine's food section, Muhlke used the term to encompass food blogs as well as memoirs about eating, cooking, and traveling. Beyond its broadness, the usefulness of "foodoir" (Muhlke 2009) as a descriptor is limited by its obvious pun on the French word for bedroom, "boudoir," which suggests its relevance is limited only to texts that use food as a tool for seduction.

What distinguishes the memoir with recipes as a genre from other forms of life writing is its capacity for mimicry and dynamism in the opportunity the texts offer for readers to test their own palates against those of the writers. Unlike more traditional autobiographies, which narrate compelling life events particular to the person who experienced them, memoirs with recipes discuss specific stages or aspects of the writer's life that are somehow punctuated by his or her memories about eating specific types of meals. These immigrant memoirs, thus, are not focused exclusively on food, but they do allow for an unprecedented level of readerly interaction with the text through the inclusion of recipes. By following these and preparing the dishes featured within their pages, readers can indeed share gustatory pleasures comparable to those of the writer: they can enjoy the same aromas, and taste the very flavor combinations that epitomize the author's recollection of any given meal. This is not to say that the reader can "eat" the writer in the way that Smith and Watson feared would happen with "gastrographies." Even if they do not actually cook from these books, readers can still rely on their innate ability to recall the exact taste of ingredients, what James Beard, the dean of American cooking, called "taste memory" (Beard 2001, 4), and use this embodied experience to compare their own food preferences to those of the writer. This type of comparison based on actual taste or those conjured from memory allows for a more complex, fuller appreciation of the subject matter under discussion than is possible with other types of life writing in which the reader's identification with the protagonist is aspirational at best.

No matter the degree to which recipes are only approximations of a real dish, the recipes' role in the context of these memoirs is to lend an air of authenticity to the claims writers make about incidents in their past. According to the U.S. Copyright office, U.S. law does not cover recipes that are "mere listings of ingredients." Whereas cookbooks typically undergo rigorous recipe testing before publication to ensure a consistent yield and predictable results, food memoirs with recipes make no claims for either originality or duplicability of the recipes they include beyond the implied endorsement of the writers' pleasant memories of eating such meals. In that regard, their truth-value is akin to that of other primary documents that support memory work, like photographs. I owe this insight to Hirsch's discussion of the malleability of photographs as archival objects, what she calls the "contradictions of the archives we have inherited," because "archival photographic images appear in postmemorial texts in altered form: they are cropped, enlarged, projected onto other images; they are reframed and de- or re-contextualized; they are embedded in new narratives, new texts; they are surrounded by new frames" (Hirsch 2012, 68). As primary sources, both recipes and photographs lend themselves to manipulation by the very people who tout their supposedly inherent value as evidence of their account of the past: they can be altered, photographs through framing, cropping, or resizing, and recipes through substitution of ingredients or a change in the method of preparation. Unlike photographs printed in books, however, recipes lend themselves to further manipulation and appropriation by the tome's readers, who can choose to follow or modify them and then enjoy the results.

Methodology and Critical Framework

Despite the wide availability of free recipe archives on the internet, food memoirs with recipes have proven to be remarkably popular, generating substantial sales and earning rave reviews. Their success is due in part to the fact that quite a few of the writers I discuss—among them, novelists Austin Clarke, Diana Abu-Jaber, and Denise Chávez; poet Maya Angelou; playwrights Eduardo Machado and Ntozake Shange; and cookbook writers Madhur Jaffrey and Colette Rossant—address themselves to an existing reader base familiar with their previous publications. My analysis of this literary subgenre focuses on the memory work that specific individuals undertake when they share their personal recollections of significant circumstances in their eating lives related to the family's history of immigration. The texts also chronicle the power struggles that take place behind closed doors as the family unit negotiates how to adapt old, and adopt new, traditions at the table. I used the following criteria to guide my selection of texts for this archive. The memoirs under discussion all share some common features:

1. they include actual recipes for specific dishes;
2. they make immigration a defining part of their narrative; and
3. they focus primarily on home cooking rather than discussing the professional aspect of cooking in the restaurant or catering businesses.

This first criterion immediately ruled out such lush and evocative texts as Bich Minh Nguyen's *Stealing Buddha's Dinner* (2007) and Louise DeSalvo's *Crazy in the Kitchen: Food, Feuds, and Forgiveness in an Italian American Family* (2004), both of which discuss the importance of food to the processes of immigration, acculturation, and assimilation without, however, incorporating actual recipes. The emphasis on immigration as a second criterion ruled out discussing memoirs by James Beard, Calvin Trilling, M. F. K. Fisher, Julia Child, and Ruth Reichl, none of whom discuss their respective families' immigration histories, despite their immense contribution to popularizing the memoir as a compelling genre through which to explain the significance of food to their personal and professional lives. By privileging home cooking rather than fine dining as its third criterion, this study leaves out professional chefs who have published memoirs with recipes, even if they themselves were immigrants or the children of immigrants. The only exception to this rule is the brief discussion in chapter 3 of Chef Edward Lee's *Smoke and Pickles* (2013), which sets the stage for my reading of the emergence of a new South whose foodways are undergoing some serious reinvention.

Though they discuss cooking, the writers of these memoirs primarily depict themselves as "eating subjects" marked in some way by immigration; this identity category conflates the remembered delight of sampling a particular dish at a specific point in time, and the anticipation of reliving that same pleasure in the future. My use of this term is indebted to Elspeth Probyn's scholarship on the relation between food, sex, and gender as these affect the process of identity formation. Probyn's concept of "alimentary identities" (Probyn 2000, 24) refers to how people's habitual choices about food reveal something about their self-understanding and sense of belonging to multiple, and sometimes overlapping, segments of society. Since the memoirs with recipes under discussion focus more on the writers' enjoyment of specific meals in the past, rather than analyzing their contemporary eating preferences, I use the concept of the "eating subject" to encompass the totality of each writer's eating acts as recalled in these texts. Clarke, Abu-Jaber, Chávez, Angelou, Shange, Machado, Jaffrey, Rossant, and the other writers I discuss frame their specific food choices as springboards for explorations of the degree to which their own, or their parents', experience of immigration has impacted their sense of belonging and being accepted into American society. Finally, through its investigation of how immigrants feel about the food choices facing them, *The Immigrant Kitchen* facilitates an exploration of American foodways as they appear to immigrants since, as Krishnendu Ray points out, "what is more intriguing and less studied is the attitude of immigrants toward the host culture and, in particular, their reading of American food" (Ray 2004, 109). This view is not always positive, and by contrasting the intergenerational perspectives on this topic, this study aims to analyze the resistance to assimilation as much as its acceptance among half-immigrants and their forbears.

The Chapters

In order to facilitate comparison, I have grouped texts according to common themes rather than relying on the featured writers' national background as the organizing principle for each section, since such a strategy would have the unintended effect of rendering the individual chapters as de facto ethnic enclaves.

The first chapter, "From Academic Sojourners to Settler Migrants: 'Scholarship Boy' and Girls in the Kitchen," considers texts penned by immigrant writers born in former British colonies that maintain political affiliations as part of the Commonwealth of Nations: Barbadian novelist Austin Clarke (*Pig Tails 'n Breadfruit*, 1999), Indian food writer Madhur Jaffrey (*Climbing the Mango Trees: A Memoir of a Childhood in India*, 2007), and Singaporean journalist Cheryl Lu-Lien Tan (*A Tiger in the Kitchen: A Memoir of Food and Family*, 2011). I apply the term "scholarship boy," first articulated by British sociologist Richard Hoggart in his landmark study, *The Uses of Literacy* (1957), to this group of bright colonial subjects whose own impressive academic achievements gained them entry into universities abroad. Originally, the term referred to white, lower-class, male British subjects who did well in school and earned the opportunity to study in more rigorous and prestigious academic institutions in England. Clarke studied in Canada; Jaffrey in the mother country, Britain; while Tan earned her undergraduate degree from a private university in the United States.

The chapter contends that these food memoirs pursue a postcolonial reframing of their respective writers' colonial childhoods, such that the development of each memoirist's culinary skills is discussed in light of his or her academic achievements in the United States. Therefore, *Pig Tails 'n Breadfruit*, *Climbing the Mango Trees*, and *A Tiger in the Kitchen* all establish that their respective authors have acquired the competencies associated with higher education in the metropolitan center without losing sight of their roots and place of origin. The stigma of "selling out" is one of the risks inherent in accepting the scholarship, just as the lure of "going native" due to an intimate association with the local culture was an ever-present threat during the era of European colonial expansion. Though they initially arrive in Western metropoles as "sojourners," the "scholarship boy" and girls eventually change their status and become settler migrants who choose to make their lives their new homeland. Thus, these memoirs' combined emphasis on academic and culinary achievement ends up promoting a specific view of immigrants as people who, in Krishendu Ray's terms, "play out the Orientalist argument in reverse" (Ray 2004, 110) by bestowing the gift of "Culture," in this case figured as recipes, upon their new homelands, instead of coming empty-handed in search of the American (or Canadian, in Clarke's case) dream.

The second chapter, "Eating in Public as Performance of Assimilation, Diaspora, or Ethnic Belonging," examines the competing social pressures American-born children of immigrant parents face from both their peers and their families. These memoirs depict two types of public eating scenarios: children eating "smelly" or exotic food alongside peers and frenemies in the school cafeteria, and grown children accompanying their parents to their homeland and being asked to dine with other natives or locals. I compare discussions of public eating in Linda Furiya's *Bento Box in the Heartland: My Japanese Girlhood in Whitebread America* (2006), Diana Abu-Jaber's *The Language of Baklava* (2005), Leslie Li's *Daughter of Heaven: A Memoir with Earthly Recipes* (2005), and Colette Rossant's first two memoirs, *Apricots on the Nile* (2004a) and *Return to Paris* (2004b). Anita Mannur's notion of "culinary citizenship" comes into play in my analysis of the emotional trauma Furiya, Abu-Jaber, Li, and Rossant experience in their struggle to earn the approval of both peers and family members through the eating performances in which they engage.

Although immigrant status cannot be inherited, the domestic sphere becomes inherently transnational in these memoirs. The roles of cultural insider and outsider alternate depending on the context. Within the domestic sphere, immigrant parents define the family's values by holding their children to the codes of conduct prized in their country of origin, which are often at odds with mainstream American expectations for children's behavior and enjoyment of leisure. In public settings in the United States, the American-born children of immigrant families show greater mastery of, and fluency in, the dominant society's rules of etiquette, including the gastronomic lexicon of inoffensive meals for public consumption, which, if violated, results in racial and ethnic slurs aimed at shaming people into compliance of social expectations. As soon as these writers travel to the ancestral homeland, however, they cease being the experts and experience the disorientation of occupying a subject position as a cultural outsider. The parents show off their adult children's enjoyment of traditional foods as proof that they have successfully raised "American" children who nonetheless know where they come from. Because of their communal nature, then, public meals enforce the normalization of the prevailing cultural and gastronomic forms, and deviations from these norms have the potential to embarrass or shame those who commit them.

The third chapter, "Mapping the New South(west)ern Home," analyzes how African Americans and Latinos are imbricated into the distinctive cultures of the New South though their respective ethnic/national culinary traditions: soul food, Southwestern, and Caribbean. The writers discussed in this section interweave their personal genealogies with larger historical forces—from their roots in European colonialism and its involvement with transatlantic slavery, to the internal displacements of both Manifest Destiny and the Great Migration, to the wave of new immigrants that arrived during the Cold War. My thinking about the South as a mythical space is influenced by the work of two historians: James N. Gregory, whose *The Southern Diaspora* discusses the multiple histories of the Great Migration, and Christopher Morris's *Becoming Southern*, which emphasizes the evolution of the South as a concept as well as a geographical region. Memoirs discussed in the chapter include poet Maya Angelou's *Hallelujah! The Welcome Table* (2004), Patty Pinner's *Sweets: Soul Food Desserts & Memoirs* (2003), cookbook writer Mary Urrutia Randelman's *Memories of a Cuban Kitchen* (1992), newspaper food columnist Viviana Carballo's *Havana Salsa: Stories and Recipes* (2006), playwright Eduardo Machado's *Tastes Like Cuba: An Exile's Hunger for Home* (2007), and novelist Denise Chávez's *A Taco Testimony: Meditations on Family, Food and Culture* (2006). These memoirs include recipes for dishes that simultaneously typify the national cuisine of the family's country of origin and also serve as "authentic" representations of a regionally inflected way of being part of the New South.

I owe my reading of the impact of recent immigration to the New South to Chef Edward Lee's evocative contribution to this genre, *Smoke and Pickles: Recipes and Stories from a New Southern Kitchen* (2013), which reads like a love letter to his adopted region. Lee's account of the charming hospitality he received after moving to Kentucky from New York, especially as the child of Korean immigrants, spoke to a new openness to diversity rather than a preservation of Old Dixie. I put this argument to the test in the chapter by recasting Cuban immigration to Miami in a new light, not as an isolated migration to escape Communism, but rather as a herald of a Caribbean resettlement pattern that has only continued to grow since the end of the twentieth century.[6] The chapter ends with a reading of how Mexican food

---

6. New waves of Caribbean immigrants have continued to arrive and settle down in Florida, with Haitians and Puerto Ricans both looking for more economic opportunity than is available on their respective islands. The Community Survey of the U.S. Census Bureau numbers the population of Haitians in the United States who live in Florida at above 100,000. See Buchanan, Albert, and Beaulieu, 2010. According to

is at the center of disputes between various Mexican American regional traditions—New Mexican and Texan, for example—even as other ethnicities, like Cubans and African Americans, feel no compunction in sharing their own recipes for Mexican food.

The fourth chapter, "Expats in Love: Recipes for Belonging Abroad," considers how the memoirists' culinary performances of ethnic belonging to the United States become even more complicated once they take residence abroad. The memoirs discussed in this chapter chronicle the protagonists' romantic and gastronomic adventures as American women abroad who find themselves relegated to the domestic sphere of the household while their partners work and engage actively within established, international business networks. Philosopher Lisa Heldke's work on "food adventurers" and Kristin Ramsdell's analysis of the romance fiction genre constitute the critical foundation through which I analyze the narrative strategies these expatriates pursue in their accounts of eating and cooking abroad. I return to French-born cookbook author Colette Rossant, who recounts her stint living in Tanzania with her American husband and youngest child in *The World in My Kitchen: The Adventures of a (Mostly) French Woman in America* (2006), and then compare her stable married life to three more tempestuous love stories. These are from Korean adoptee and food writer Kim Sunée, who chronicles the course of her romance and breakup with the founder of L'Occitane beauty products in *Trail of Crumbs: Hunger, Love, and the Search for Home* (2008); the second volume of Linda Furiya's memoirs *How to Cook a Dragon* (2008), which tells the parallel narratives of how she learned to cook authentic Chinese meals in Beijing while living with the man she would eventually marry and divorce; and Chinese American journalist Jen Lin-Liu, whose engagement, marriage, and pregnancy serve as the backstories to both volumes of her memoirs, *Serve the People* (2008) and *On The Noodle Road: From Beijing to Rome with Love and Pasta* (2013).

These writers' shared status as ethnic or naturalized expatriates means they discuss the difficulties of maintaining an "American" cultural and gastronomic identity that is geographically situated and temporally oriented. Their residence abroad is often, though not exclusively, facilitated by their romantic involvement with the men in their lives, though these memoirs are not simply panegyrics to the new-found glories of domestic bliss. Instead, I contend that by framing their culinary discoveries of new cuisines alongside

---

Hunter College's Center for Puerto Rican Studies, in 2010, "Puerto Rican population growth in the United States is driven by its growth in the South, and the state and metropolitan areas of Florida are driving the population growth in the South" (Vargas-Ramos and García-Ellín 2013, 3).

the progress they make toward realizing their own professional goals as writers thanks to their economic privilege and distance from daily life in the United States, this group of memoirs emerges as a feminist meditation upon the compromises women make in order to pursue their dreams of family and/or career.

The fifth chapter, "Diasporic Inventions: Reclaiming Family Culinary Traditions," follows three self-declared "diasporics," in the terms of postcolonial scholar Betty Joseph (2012), as they choose to reclaim a culinary family heritage that was not passed down to them. This chapter is organized around the theme of the familial holiday traditions, and examines the impact that the major life transition of becoming a parent has on the memoirists' sense of what is important. I use Stephan Palmié's concept of "gastrographical revisionism" (Palmié 2009), which refers to purposeful rewritings of a culinary event or tradition to fit into larger narratives of national (or religious) belonging to analyze the stakes of the memoirs' suggestions that readers invest the holiday season with more personal meaning through the adoption of new, or reclamation of traditional, culinary rituals. In this chapter, I turn to two distinct but related archives—memoirs with recipes and how-to manuals for celebrating these "invented" diasporic traditions (in Eric Hobsbawm's terms).

Whether by mere coincidence or through some gendered stylistic preference, the holiday manuals-cum-memoirs discussed here, which show the masses how to properly observe specific traditions, are all written by men, including novelist Jonathan Safran Foer's beautifully crafted *New American Haggadah* (2012), journalist Eric V. Copage's *Kwanzaa: An African-American Celebration of Culture and Cooking* (1991), and television writer Daniel O'Keefe's humorous *Seinfeld* spinoff, *The Real Festivus: The True Story Behind America's Favorite Made-Up Holiday* (2005). I put these manuals in direct conversation with the memoirs that best correspond to their overall goals. Thus, a good foil for Foer is Elizabeth Ehrlich, whose *Miriam's Kitchen: A Memoir* (1997) chronicles her transition to keeping a kosher home in honor of her Orthodox Jewish mother-in-law, a Holocaust survivor. In contrast, novelist and playwright Ntozake Shange decides to incorporate dishes eaten at many different outposts of the African diaspora into her cooking repertoire after learning new recipes from her family and friends, as she explains in *If I Can Cook / You Know God Can* (1998). This diasporic practice is in keeping with the Afrocentric rationale behind the creation of Kwanzaa as a new holiday, which Copage celebrates. Finally, O'Keefe's postmodern and multimodal Festivus is a great foil for Anya Von Bremzen's tongue-in-cheek recreations of "fake" or inauthentic Soviet holiday traditions in *Mastering the*

Art of Soviet Cooking (2013). This volume chronicles her effort to come to terms with the artificial culinary lore promoted by the Soviet government of her youth from the vantage point of her decades in exile in the United States.

The book concludes with "Talking Turkey: The Thanksgiving Holiday as the Measure of Assimilation," a brief overview of popular Hollywood films depicting immigrant characters celebrating their first Thanksgiving. I consider how *Avalon* (1990), the epic story of a Russian Jewish family's arrival in America and its gradual assimilation throughout the generations, is encapsulated in one testy Thanksgiving meal when the family members who have moved to the suburbs start eating before the city-dwelling family patriarch arrives. Chaos ensues, and the family rift only intensifies from there. Alternatively, two more recent films present multicultural Thanksgiving celebrations that portend better integration of fellow citizens at different stages of assimilating, reclaiming their heritage, or entering into interracial courtships: the West Coast version of intersecting ethnic lives, *What's Cooking?* (2000), and the East Coast version of interracial collaboration, *Pieces of April* (2003). Although they are unfailingly positive in their outlooks, both *Pieces of April* and *What's Cooking?* confront the "darker" side of this all-American holiday, through suggestions of crime, intolerance, and prejudice. Each is tackled head-on, for the most part, and accepted as real but not a defining aspect of day-to-day life in large urban centers. Instead, all three films celebrate the power of a ritual meal, duplicated in households all across the nation, to cement a sense of shared mission, identity, and common weal.

Whereas this book began by considering how mastering one's native foodways is a key marker of an immigrant's individual success and evidence of his or her aptitude for starting life afresh upon distant shores, it ends by noting the impulse to reconnect with one's transnational diasporic networks as a source of comfort and continuity. There is no one simple story of immigration, acculturation, and displacement told through food. Instead, the memoirs discussed throughout *The Immigrant Kitchen* welcome their readers into the heart of the domestic realm and show them the hospitality of breaking bread together, if only virtually.

Chapter 1

From Academic Sojourners to Settler Migrants

"Scholarship Boy" and Girls in the Kitchen

Barbadian novelist Austin Clarke's *Pig Tails 'n Breadfruit*, Indian cookbook writer and actress Madhur Jaffrey's *Climbing the Mango Trees: A Memoir of a Childhood in India*, and Singaporean food writer Cheryl Lu-Lien Tan's *A Tiger in the Kitchen: A Memoir of Food and Family* interweave accounts of the writers' academic success with references to their individual journeys toward mastery of the home-cooking traditions of their countries of origin. The more accolades these postcolonial subjects achieved in formal schooling situations and the further afield their studies took them, the greater need Clarke, Jaffrey, and Tan felt to connect with the cultures they left behind by learning to prepare the dishes they associated with their home countries. By juxtaposing or contrasting recollections of their formal liberal arts and informal culinary educations, Clarke, Jaffrey, and Tan suggest home cooking is part of one's well-rounded cultural citizenship. Though they have long been immigrants to the United States or Canada, these writers continue to think of themselves as "worthy" or "gifted" postcolonial subjects who attribute their current success to their earlier achievement as students and scholarship recipients.

In describing their years as young scholars with student visas and institutional funding via scholarships in *Pig Tails 'n Breadfruit*, *Climbing the Mango Trees*, and *A Tiger in the Kitchen*, Clarke, Jaffrey, and Tan thus leverage the cachet associated with their academic pedigrees into a kind of "respectable exoticism" (Nance 2002, 624) that explains their difference from mainstream culture. They claim the authority of cultural ambassadors, well poised to communicate effectively with an interested reading audience from their adopted homelands. All share a common cultural legacy of imperialism manifested most clearly through the British-style colonial education they received, which tracked children by ability based on their performance of a series of high-stakes exams.

This chapter explores the intersections between education and displacement by employing British sociologist Richard Hoggart's concept of "the scholarship boy" and the term "academic sojourner" as developed by John L. Cox. Together, these work as the critical lens through which to understand Clarke's, Jaffrey's, and Tan's food memoirs with recipes. "Scholarship boys" (Hoggart 2008) and, by extension, scholarship girls, face both external and internal pressures to conform to their overlapping communities (family, gender, school, nation), even as they pursue educational opportunities outside of their home countries. The term "academic sojourner" (Cox 1988) has become widely accepted in the field of international education studies. Cox draws a useful distinction between "settler" migrants, who spend their lives in their new homelands, and "sojourners," who plan only a temporary stay in a foreign country. Only later, and probably in large part due to the success of their academic sojourn abroad, do Clarke, Jaffrey, and Tan become settler migrants who decide to put down permanent roots in a new country and change their nationality. I apply these concepts to encompass both the academic and culinary achievements of the postcolonial men and women who have become published food writers. These texts mark the turning point when these writers begin to recognize themselves as transplants, no longer displaced or living abroad, but full-fledged members of a new country.

While these three authors share the experience of academic success and the displacement from their birthplace it inherently demands, they do not share a uniformly privileged background. Clarke grew up in a modest household, the first child of a single mother who later married and had other children, and celebrates the long and painful history of Bajan (Barbadian) national cuisine by calling it "slave food." In contrast, Jaffrey and Tan hail from privileged social circumstances within their respective societies—defined by caste or ethnic group as well as financial resources. Jaffrey informs readers that her family "were a subcaste of Hindus known as Kaysthas" (2007, 12), a warrior class. Cheryl Lu-Lien Tan explains that as Singaporeans of Han Chinese ancestry, she and her family occupied a highly privileged position within this stratified society. Clarke's, Jaffrey's, and Tan's track records of academic achievement afforded them the opportunity to pursue educational opportunities in the West with the financial support of various scholarship systems. Some of these were set up to enable students from former British colonies to study in the Western metropoles of the Commonwealth, like Clarke did at the University of Toronto, Canada, and Jaffrey at the Royal Academy of Dramatic Arts in London, England. In the United States, private schools' global outreach efforts benefitted Cheryl Lu-Lien Tan, who graduated from Northwestern University.

In *The Migrant's Table*, Krishnendu Ray explains that his choice of a similar demographic, affluent middle-class Bengali households in the United States, as the subjects of his ethnographic/sociological analysis was warranted because this group of migrants "is often a protagonist of globalization" (Ray 2004, 7). Most of the subjects in Ray's study are members of large diasporic communities, whereas Clarke, Jaffrey, and Tan all present themselves as individuals to their readers. Despite the disparities in the socioeconomic backgrounds, their shared status as academic sojourners and scholarship recipients is what first made them into "protagonist[s] of globalization," something on which their memoirs capitalize as further proof of their "respectable exoticism." By the time of their memoirs' publication, however, all three writers had achieved a measure of economic security in the United States and Canada, thanks to the success of their own careers.

Pig Tails 'n Breadfruit, Climbing the Mango Trees, and *A Tiger in the Kitchen* all portray academic and culinary educations as equally important, if asynchronous, factors contributing to the writers' transition from childhood into adulthood, and from academic sojourner into settler migrants. While the academic scholarships these writers earned through hours of study, rote memorization, and focus under pressure during their schooling facilitated their entry to the West, none of them chose to pursue the civil service or government careers into which their performance in the British school system's exams provided automatic entry, though Clarke spent a brief time as an adviser to the Bajan prime minister. They also did not apply the skills they honed in college to careers in academia. Instead, the liberal arts education Tan received as an undergraduate student at Northwestern University, and that the rest of the group acquired at the postgraduate level in their respective universities, prepared them to pursue creative freelance opportunities in fields like acting (Jaffrey), journalism (Tan), and literature (Clarke). As each of them mined the quotidian aspects of their personal histories for larger, universal dimensions that not only make good stories but also bring people together around a table to eat, these writers relied upon the critical thinking skills at the core of their Western education.

Though they all lack formal culinary training, in their books they assume the role of cooking instructors enlightening North American readers about the significance of food in daily life and customs in Barbados, India, and Singapore, respectively. At the end of their illustrious careers, Clarke and Jaffrey turn back to an examination of their student days as a way to recover the flavors of their youth. In contrast, Cheryl Lu-lien Tan briefly mentions her schooling as she launched her new food-centric career, pausing to share the lessons she learned from her youthful mistakes, both in and out of the kitchen. Despite their success in the classroom, Clarke, Jaffrey, and Tan all celebrate the authentic human relations they experienced in the domestic space as a corrective to the grooming and molding they underwent in the vaunted halls of academe. In this same vein, as writers they cultivate a dynamic relationship with the audience, championing the notion that anyone who reads their work can also learn to prepare the meals that made their home life so special. Clarke, Jaffrey, and Tan set out to teach their readers without subjecting them to an education per se. Reading and eating remain social pleasures in these memoirs. Together, *Pig Tails 'n Breadfruit, Climbing the Mango Trees,* and *A Tiger in the Kitchen* make it clear that culinary knowledge is an especially appealing type of cultural capital for both sojourners and settler migrants to accrue.

The "Scholarship Boy" as Template for Achievement

Britain's stratified social system was a key factor in the development of a scholarship system that structured opportunities for upward mobility for the best and brightest young men, who could then assume civil servant and other mid-level professional positions. This system proved so successful it was expanded internationally. Richard Hoggart first articulated his thoughts on the dilemma faced by bright, working-class young men whose success in the classroom facilitated their individual upward mobility in his landmark study, *The Uses of Literacy.* Speaking from experience as someone from humble origins who rose through the ranks to become a career academic, Hoggart himself challenged the elitism of the institution wherein he made his livelihood by being a serious advocate for the study of popular and contemporary culture. In so doing, Hoggart not only inaugurated the groundbreaking Birmingham School of cultural studies, but also made the case for a real analysis of the costs—emotional and psychological—that an education beyond their means puts upon those working-class children selected to pursue opportunities unavailable to their peers or family members.

Hoggart's original "scholarship boy" was a white, lower-class, male British subject whose outstanding performance in school exams earned him scholarships to fund his university and postgraduate studies. This system made it possible for bright, disadvantaged young men to climb to the managerial or professional classes and become doctors, lawyers, or bankers.

Rather than discredit the entire system that facilitates upward mobility in England, Hoggart focused his critique on the system's impact on the majority of the young men who demonstrated a precocious talent for testing well but lacked the innate drive or talents to break out of the mid-level positions for which their studies primed them. As he contended, these subjects found themselves alienated from their humble beginnings and unable to fit comfortably into the social class to which their early academic success provided entry. Hoggart suggested that the sacrifices these bright young men made in order to maintain the outstanding academic performance that earned the scholarship set in motion a process of isolation and alienation that took root early in their lives and quickly led them to a crossroads even within the geography of their own home. Their heavy homework loads relegated these boys to the female domestic spaces of the household, like the kitchen, where they completed their assignments under the mother's supervision. This situation hampered their chances for social interaction outside with their peers who had free time for sports or other pastimes; the resulting physical separation from peers and/or siblings thus increased the isolation felt by the "scholarship boys":

> But these are the male groups among which others in his generation grew up, and his detachment from them is emotionally linked with one more aspect of his home situation—that he now tends to be closer to the women of the house than to the men. This is true, even if his father is not the kind who dismisses books and reading as "a woman's game." The boy spends a large part of his time at the physical centre of the home, where the women's spirit rules, quietly getting on with his work whilst his mother gets on with her jobs—the father not yet back from work or out for a drink with his mates. (Hoggart 2008, 227–28)

In Hoggart's view, this proximity to women like his mother did not inherently feminize the "scholarship boy," who, after all, attended to the intellectual labor of "his work" while she was occupied by her more physical toil of "her jobs"; however, entry into the world of male leisure, like fraternizing at the pub or playing outside with his brothers, was denied to him precisely because of the focus and concentration demanded by his studies. This reading of the "moderately endowed" (Hoggart 2008, 226) boy as a welcomed interloper or a pampered visitor into the female spaces of the family home inverts the logic of empire by establishing the domestic "center" as the social periphery, and the margins of the home—the outside world—as the normative middle, the axis of power and validation.

Since the idea of "the scholarship boy" entered into common parlance, it has been transformed beyond its original parameters and claimed as a badge of identity by luminaries from across the former British colonies. While the dedication, sacrifice, and discipline required to pass the British exam system were promoted as strong character traits, those claiming this identity in a postcolonial context just as often embrace the title of "scholarship boy" as a means of indicting the system that attempted to erase or devalue the markers of class, ethnicity, and culture in the interest of cultivating a "British" sensibility.

According to Hilary Perralton's *Learning Abroad: A History of the Commonwealth Scholarship and Fellowship Plan*, the Commonwealth Scholarship and Fellowship Plan (CSFP), which was inaugurated in 1960, applied to both male and female students and was formulated with the aim of facilitating collaboration and intellectual exchange among countries of the Commonwealth:

> Governments have used scholarships within a political agenda that goes beyond the educational one. In the early discussions about CSFP, Commonwealth cohesion was seen as one of its driving forces. Both Britain and Canada have demonstrated their continuing commitment to Commonwealth ties by recruiting students from the industrialised as well as the developing Commonwealth, treating the plan for much of its history as being in some ways different from an aid programme. (Perralton 2009, 27)

The CSFP probably allocated the fellowships Austin Clarke and Madhur Jaffrey received to their respective countries. As former British colonies and members of the Commonwealth of Nations, Barbados and India stood to benefit from participating in such scholarship programs, which had the potential to pay dividends well beyond those of a traditional "aid programme." The expectation was that Canada and Britain would train professionals who would then return home and take up leadership roles in their countries of origin, thereby creating and eventually sustaining a stable local leadership structure. Clarke did spend some time working for the Barbadian government in its embassy in Washington, DC, but both he and Jaffrey have done more to serve their respective countries of origin by earning acclaim for their artistic performances—he for his writing, and she for her acting and cookbooks.

Tan's scholarship to a university in the United States was not part and parcel of an international "aid programme," but rather the product of the fractured scholarship system that underwrites American academia. The financial award package she received was not linked to earning a particular score on a British exam, but instead was funded by the revenue raised by the philanthropic networks of alumni and donors who contribute money to colleges and universities. American universities often admit international students to enhance their own global education efforts, as well as make their campuses more diverse. By developing an international alumni base, institutions of higher learning hope to broaden the scope of their influence internationally and continue to attract high-quality students in the future. Like Clarke and Jaffrey before her, however, Tan has earned acclaim and attention for her home country through the publication of her food memoir with recipes.

The Classroom at the "Centre of the Home"

All three writers recall instances similar to the scenario Hoggart sketches out for the studious "scholarship boy" whose mother keeps him company, and suggest that the kitchen was the academic and nutritional center of their respective homes. As a child in Barbados, Austin Clarke learned the art of cooking directly from his mother, in kitchens both inside the house and outside in the backyard. In patriarchal societies, such as that of 1940s Barbados, this mode of direct transmission of domestic knowledge from parent to child usually follows along gendered lines. As the only child of a single mother for the majority of his childhood, however, Clarke had no qualms about spending time in the kitchen. In the introduction to *Pig Tails 'n Breadfruit*, Clarke alternates between pledging his ongoing identification with his mother's way of thinking about food on the one hand, and on the other, betraying that same worldview through the very act of writing down Bajan food recipes in the memoir, however informally, for the edification of complete strangers. He informs his audience that the Barbadian women whose culinary ingenuity he praises in this memoir would construe both the readers' reliance on books to learn culinary lore, as well as his own complicity in producing such a volume, as tantamount to culinary blasphemy or treason:

> There was never, and still is not, a cookbook in my mother's house.
>
> In this idea of having to be shown how to cook from the pages of a book lies an ineradicable assault upon the culture and character of Barbadian women. Instead, both culture and the ability of a woman to handle herself in the kitchen are based upon the handing down through time of methods of cooking. Things handed down must be remembered, word for word, so as not to dilute "the way of cooking"; and in this way they are expected to retain their essential essence of perfection and legitimacy. (Clarke 1999, 4)

In this passage, Clarke adopts the role of cultural translator, explaining the bygone world of his youth for the enlightenment and edification of his Canadian and American readers. By the time of the memoir's publication, Clarke's mother had immigrated to the United States, so this notion of a specifically female, Barbadian way of passing down culinary knowledge has not only crossed gender boundaries when articulated by Clarke as an adult male, but it has also become diasporic while maintaining a cultural identification with Barbados that lasts despite his mother's own immigrant status.

Rather than follow contemporary recipe conventions, Clarke's prominent use of Bajan dialect and constant explanations of cultural mores in *Pig Tails 'n Breadfruit* harkens back to an earlier model used to record "receipts" in use in North American cookbooks and books of household management dating back to the eighteenth century.[1] The "receipt" format was concise; the ingredients and procedures were all condensed into one paragraph, unadorned by any flourish, and followed by another and yet another. Space on the page was at a premium, so what mattered was the quantity of the recipes included in a volume, not how aesthetically pleasing the typesetting was. Clarke shares his mother's recipes and those of the women around him as he was growing up using the receipt model with some specific modifications:

1. The recipes in *Pig Tails* feature frequent narrative digressions and banter between the narrator and his readers, including Clarke's assumptions of what reader reactions to his comments would be.

---

[1]. The more utilitarian receipt style of recipe writing was only discontinued in the second decade of the twentieth century. The other writers discussed in this book follow the more modern stylistic conventions for recipe writing format: each states the name of the dish or meal, followed by a list of ingredients and measurements, and then a numbered list of steps or procedures the cook must follow in order to prepare the meal.

2. Ingredient lists, measurements, and specific cooking techniques (or their contemporary equivalents) are all there to be found, but a recipe like the one for "bakes" takes five pages to unfold, and includes a detailed discussion of the proper day of the week in which it should be prepared (Sundays) and for what kind of company: "the high and mighty in society" (Clarke 1999, 49).

This vernacular approach approximates the discursive nature of actual interpersonal communication in the kitchen; Clarke's digressions into gossipy insights into local customs and ways to determine who is and is not a good cook echo the types of conversations women in Clarke's circle must have had as they labored over hot pots or washed dishes.

Clarke's memoir is structured chronologically, from his birth to his adulthood, and moves geographically from his mother's house in Barbados in the opening pages to her home in the United States in its last chapter. Though he frequently inserts tangential asides in which he taunts, teases, and goads his Canadian readers into cooking the dishes he describes, Clarke is somewhat reticent about discussing his university studies or subsequent life in Canada. However, when he finally discusses his half-siblings, as he does in the concluding chapter, where they all cook together in their mother's kitchen in Mount Laurel, New Jersey, he immediately identifies them by their academic pedigrees:

> My three brothers—one a graduate of John Jay Law College, working now as a carpenter, another a medical student, the third an airline pilot—and I cooked enough food to feed an army, an expression my mother herself used to use when I was, for the first nineteen years of my life, the only child in the house. Back then, it was a smaller house, with no barbecue pit, no swimming pool, no two-car garage, no "motto-car." But the kitchen was almost half the side of our house, and her instructions about cooking were sharp and stentorian. She assumed that parental, superior attitude that left no possibility of independence of variation, of personal assurance, because my assurance was hers, my self-assurance came from her dignity of meaning, and from her memory of that history and her understanding of the myths that surround our ways of cooking. (Clarke 1999, 245–46)

Thus, not only does *Pig Tails 'n Breadfruit* engage in a bit of national masquerading by flattening the differences between Canada and the United States, but it also uses the latter to signify the opposite of everything that conveys Bajan food and culture. Though he never pauses to discuss his mother's schooling, her children's success—both academic and culinary—is proof enough that her "stentorian" approach to instruction in the kitchen worked as well to produce successful men whose own academic sojourns paved the way for her New Jersey retirement.

Unlike Clarke, who knew all he needed to about cooking by the time he left his mother's home to study in Toronto, Jaffrey found that being at school away from her countrymen did a lot to temper the caste and wealth privilege of her youth: since no servants or hired cooks were around to prepare Indian meals for her at university, she had to do this herself.[2] As both an actress and a food writer, Madhur Jaffrey has earned critical acclaim by representing the complexity and charm of the cultures of her homeland for a transcontinental audience of Anglo-British fans. With the publication of her first cookbook, *An Invitation to Indian Cooking* (1973), Jaffrey began her career as a food writer, introducing herself to readers through explicit references to her place within the U.S. educational system as a mother constantly "approached at parties and P.T.A. meetings by a fresh breed of enthusiastic Americans" (Jaffrey 1973, 3). As an organization, the Parent Teacher Association (PTA) occupies a privileged place in American popular culture; this group is best known for the bake sales they host in schools across the nation to raise money so teachers can purchase supplies for their students and thereby enhance learning. This organization also represents the unofficial social structures that mark or delimit acceptability and belonging in the local school community. Jaffrey's membership in the PTA simultaneously establishes her cooking bona fides as an "American" mother in a way her readers can immediately understand. Decades later, now at the pinnacle of her career, Jaffrey decides to engage in "respectable exoticism" through the publication of her memoir, *Climbing the Mango Trees*. She wants her faithful followers to see her in a more innocent light, as a young, carefree Indian student herself, coming of age in the shadow of the British Empire. Only after several decades as a recognized Anglo-American authority on the many regional specialties that make up the cuisine of the subcontinent did Jaffrey combine all the autobiographical details she had already shared with readers of her various cookbooks into a single memoir with recipes, which culminates with her arrival in England as an academic sojourner, an international student.

---

2. Parama Roy and Anita Mannur offer nuanced critical readings of Jaffrey's account of learning to cook via a correspondence exchange with her mother during the time she was in school in the introduction of *An Invitation to Indian Cooking*. Their critical volumes also provide in-depth analyses of Jaffrey's treatment of issues of class, caste, nationality, and gender in the many regions of India.

In recalling memories of her childhood in colonial India, Jaffrey constructs an artificial textual universe where she imbues her idealized version of her girlhood with all the taste memory she now possesses as an adult food writer. This rhetorical and temporal disjunction is further reinforced by the presence of recipes for dishes she enjoyed at a time in her life when the kitchen held none of the allure it began to acquire once she was a lonely scholarship girl in England. One such instance that highlights the coexistence of Madhur the student and her mother within the gendered space of the home has to do with her preparation for the all-important school exams. Jaffrey explains that her mother's culinary contribution to her daughter's academic success was the preparation of "brain food" in the form of almond balls, or *badaam ki golian*. Jaffrey the cookbook writer manages to interject a recipe for this delicacy that she enjoyed as a stressed-out student:

> On most days there were two exams, with a break for lunch. Before I left in the early morning, armed with sharpened pencils, pens freshly filled with ink, ink bottles, rulers, and erasers, my mother would appear with a plate containing two almond balls (*badaam ki golian*). She made them by soaking the nuts overnight, peeling them, then grinding them with sugar and cardamom, forming soft balls, and finally covering the balls with the silver tissues. They were the most elegant two balls you could ever hope to see. My mother firmly believed that almonds were brain food, and that any child sent off to write two examination papers for six hours unfortified with almond balls was surely suffering from the grossest form of neglect. (Jaffrey 2007, 207)

This is the only "recipe" for this dish included in the book; *badaam ki golian* is not listed again in the "Family Recipes" section of *Climbing the Mango Trees*. Thus, Jaffrey's recollection of the meals from her childhood parallels the "receipt" style Austin Clarke deploys while discussing Bajan food; neither writer follows the contemporary conventions of recipe writing when discussing the meals their mothers prepared for them in their youth. In this passage, we see evidence of Jaffrey's economically privileged family incorporating her academic endeavors into the culinary logic of the household, by articulating a theory of alimentation for good parenting. This is an example of an especially intimate task, since Jaffrey explains that hired cooks usually did most of the food preparation for her extended family's household. Much like the "scholarship boy's" mother who carries out her kitchen tasks while her son does homework, Jaffrey's mother also aligns her own domestic/culinary labor with her child's "intellectual work" by making *badaam ki golian* for her children. Their shared goal is to arrive at the same result: the child's successful performance during exams. Jaffrey juxtaposes references to her educational and culinary achievements, valuing each for its potential to enrich her life personally, and also economically. In so doing, Jaffrey transforms the somewhat nostalgic tale of her (post)colonial upbringing into a narrative of feminine empowerment and cosmopolitan cultural translation for the benefit of her readers.

Like both Jaffrey and Clarke, Cheryl Lu-Lien Tan grew up in a society where schooling was modeled on the British educational system, something she describes as a good antidote to her inherent tendency toward procrastination:

> Singapore, a Commonwealth country, adopted the British school system decades ago, meaning that your entire academic career culminates in the taking of a single big exam at age eighteen. The A levels will determine which university you'll attend. Or if you'll be able to attend university at all.
>
> Now this might seem unfair to those used to the American school system, where cumulative grades and academic performance dictate your college prospects. But for someone who tends to perform best only when there's a fire ablaze under her butt, this Britty [*sic*] school system worked perfectly fine. (Tan 2011, 87)

Tan's description of the British approach to education likewise triangulates the American reader's reaction to Singapore's school system to her own, by presenting the Asian country through the prism of a familiar European framework for social organization. As the self-referential title of her memoir and the use of her full name, with elements belonging to both East and West, indicate, Cheryl Lu-Lien Tan never abandons this sense of inhabiting a double, or multiple, subject position. Tan often resorts to personal anecdote to convey to her readers the privilege enjoyed by members of the Chinese diaspora in Singapore's multiethnic society. By emphasizing rather than downplaying these differences, Tan avoids the twin pitfalls of exploiting her heritage for profit or entertainment. She embraces her contradictory impulses: her obsession with American meatloaf, her enthusiasm for mastering different techniques for baking European bread and pies, and her decision to return to her roots and rectify the omissions of her youth by finally learning to prepare all the Singaporean family dishes she enjoyed eating but never bothered to learn how to make. In this regard, Tan's girlhood experience of the kitchen closely parallels Jaffrey's.

A Tiger in the Kitchen redefines the notion of how "scholarship" girls and boys can apply the skills developed in the classroom toward new and more enriching scenarios, such as reclaiming their culinary heritage. By casting herself in the role of an amateur—not wholly ignorant of the first principles of cooking, but rather, someone with a newfound interest in mastering the many challenges of the kitchen—Tan acknowledges that the lure of academic knowledge and recognition can be hard to resist or even to balance alongside more domestic skills for career-focused women.

> Like me, the women in my mother's family were relatively slow (and reluctant) to enter the kitchen. Mum and her two sisters were a rambunctious lot for whom learning skills that would make them more marriageable (like cooking) was low on the list of priorities. Studying hard, occasionally skipping school, flirting massively with the neighborhood boys—Mum, Auntie Jane and Auntie Alice did it all. . . . Their independent streaks would eventually land them successful husbands who could afford maids to do the bulk of the cooking. Although Mum has picked up some recipes from monitoring the maid at the stove over the years, she'll be the first to tell you that her role in the kitchen remains that of the air traffic controller and not the pilot. Feeling that she had nothing to teach, she did not attempt to show me and my younger sister much beyond the go-to brownies she made whenever we were required to bring a dessert to a party and her very own version of banana bread, an oven-toasted snack of white bread topped with gobs of butter, mashed bananas, and sugar which we adored. (Tan 2011, 27–28)

By doing well academically, Cheryl followed in her mother's footsteps. This description reflects an ongoing shift from the postcolonial mind-set to a new embrace of transnational networks. The dedication of Cheryl's mother to her work over her domestic obligations reflects more international norms, which have shifted away from an adherence to strict gender roles. The kitchen is no longer a bulwark against the outside world that's threatening to change a student, as it was for Clarke's and Jaffrey's mothers. Instead, the kitchen in the Tan household was the realm of the professional cook, the maid, who makes it possible for the mother to retreat and attend to the pressures of her own career.

Although she did not spend much time in the kitchen with either her mother or the cook, Tan uses the research skills she developed as a college student when she turns to the internet to find suitable approximations of the beloved dishes she grew up eating at her grandmother's table, such as making "*tau yew bak,* a stew of pork belly braised in dark soy sauce, sweet and thick, and a mélange of spices that is the signature dish of the Teochews, the ethnic Chinese group of my paternal ancestors" (Tan 2011, 29), with the help of websites and blogs. These virtual cooking lessons don't live up to her taste memory, and Tan does not hide the mishaps she endures, sharing these culinary disasters with her readers in full detail. These kitchen failures are what propel her to fly home and learn to cook from her paternal relatives while she still has the chance to interact with them in person.

Testing One's Culinary "Authenticity"

When addressing their readers, Clarke, Jaffrey, and Tan all adopt an authoritative tone about their national cuisines because they have each had to demonstrate before a knowledgeable audience their proficiency in its preparation or, at the very least, in its consumption. Some of these cooking exams take place in school proper, while others are more metaphorical and simply refer to how the writers challenge themselves and test the seriousness of their commitment to really master the skill of home cooking. Krishnendu Ray observes the following about the relationship between immigrant nostalgia and food:

> If revisioning the landscape and insisting on an authentic meal are central to the migrant experience, so is the reimagining of time. In fact, the search for the authentic is the reversal of time. The migrant through the sheer act of abandoning the past is made more acutely aware of that betrayal. That is why she hungers to turn the present into the past. That is exactly why the migrant pours so much meaning into the rhythms of eating. That is what gives meaning—breaking up the continuum of time into intersubjectively meaningful units. Meals do that. (Ray 2004, 168)

Because they write from the subject position of settler migrants who were international students once upon a time, Clarke, Jaffrey, and Tan strategically invoke the idea of the "authentic" in order to establish some distance and difference from their readers, which is coded as "respectable exoticism" primarily because it is the sort of cultural barrier that is delicious to overcome. Together, the references to these examinations serve to establish the writers' aptitude as students who learned from their mistakes and devised strategies for mastering the tasks that at first they found difficult. They challenge the notion that there is only one correct way to prepare meals.

In *Pig Tails 'n Breadfruit,* Clarke casts himself in the role of the first-time taster of an iconic Bajan dish he never encountered as a child. Clarke's study-abroad experience as an academic sojourner eventually opened the door to permanent immigration, although that legal designation in no way deterred frequent travel "back" to the homeland each writer left behind. During one of these periods of return, Clarke served as the adviser to the prime minister (PM) of Barbados, at that time the Right Honourable Errol Walton Barrow, an instance he describes in the memoir. Summoned to the PM's home one Friday evening, Clarke arrived to find himself surrounded by fellow members of the Cabinet, all of whom had studied abroad like him and whom he describes to his readers primarily through their affiliation with particular universities or countries where they studied: Oxford, Cambridge, and Durham in the UK, or Columbia University in the United States. When everyone was called to dinner, the prime minister proudly served "privilege," a stew of okra, pig tails, and rice he had prepared. Since Clarke had never eaten this particular stew, Barrow jokingly upbraided him in public for becoming too refined by his foreign education to appreciate his country's cooking:

> Look at the big professor from a Ivy League university up in Amurca [sic], who doesn't know what privilege is! You see what happens to our biggest brains when they leave here, to go away to north Amurca [sic] and learn a lot o' foolishness? And then come back here and forget their roots? (Clarke 1999, 59)

In this situation, the prime minister adroitly encapsulated the dilemma faced by these "scholarship boys," whose education and professional achievement are perceived to have come at the expense of their knowledge and appreciation of their culture of origin. Since Clarke failed Barrow's test by not recognizing "privilege" as a canonical staple of authentic Bajan "slave food," he tried to atone by eating three servings of the stew as a way to prove his Bajan culinary citizenship to others in the group.

Both the events encapsulated in this vignette and the publication of the memoir took place long after Clarke made it as a novelist, decades after arriving in Toronto to study, and longer still after he learned to cook by helping his mother. In short, when he writes about and remembers this incident, he does so as a settler migrant to Canada. The double performances of eating "privilege" and writing about having eaten it allow Clarke to reclaim a Bajan cultural identity he had left behind in favor of a Canadian way of life. The Canadian or American readers who prepare and consume the dishes described in these pages, in contrast, would be either partaking of Canadian multiculturalism or tasting the flavors of the Commonwealth, as the case may be.

During her youth, Madhur Jaffrey attended prestigious private schools and only had to worry about exams and scholarships at the end of her high school career. She recalls with some irony how her lack of experience in the kitchen almost stymied her efforts to obtain a college education abroad. While she had applied herself in school even "through the wretched years of Partition" (Jaffrey 2007, 226), when India and Pakistan became separate countries after the official end of the British Empire's rule over the subcontinent, her education in an all-girl's school meant that she had to take a final exam not only in English and history, but also in "domestic science" (228), which somehow counted as "lower mathematics," and faced an unexpected challenge: rather than the British recipes the girls had memorized in class during the year, the final exam asked students to prepare more local fare.

> I did the best I could. I cut up everything I found—potatoes, onion, garlic, ginger, tomatoes, chilies, and green coriander—into even-sized pieces and threw them into a pot with a little water. I sprinkled a few spices and salt over the top, put the lid on, as I could not bear to look at my bubbling creation, and prayed. It did no good. The only reason I passed lower mathematics was that my marks for arithmetic were so high, they made up for the cooking I must have failed. (Jaffrey 2007, 229)

Jaffrey read the last-minute substitution of Indian ingredients for English ones as the teachers' half-hearted attempt to make the curriculum more relevant to their young Indian students. However, to her readers, it also smacks of essentialism, since the logic underlying this change implies that "good" Indian women should intuitively know how to make the food of their culture. Jaffrey's memory of her haphazard treatment of the vegetables before her constitutes an anti-recipe, meant not to be followed but to illustrate the depths of her own naiveté in the kitchen at this time. Whereas Austin Clarke might have excelled at such a task had it been part of *his* school exams, given how closely he had helped his mother in the kitchen, Madhur Jaffrey's privileged background actually worked against her in this instance since she had no direct experience upon which to draw. When faced with local ingredients not discussed in the textbook, she could neither improvise nor make do, two skills that are the hallmarks of successful home cooks. This last-minute switch conveyed the school's indecision about its educational mission: should it try to turn young Indian women into colonial versions of British housewives, or should it acknowledge the local customs and traditions? Madhur's failure in the final exam marked her as a bad student of domestic science not so much because she did not recognize how to cook the local ingredients, but rather because exposure to the art of cookery at school had not stimulated her curiosity about the more enticing foodways of her young nation, or at least of her family household. It would take time and distance from her beloved Indian cuisine during her graduate studies in England to motivate Jaffrey to learn how to cook.

The scholarship Madhur Jaffrey earned attests to her intellectual achievements and acceptance into the ranks of the meritocracy. By leaving the India of her childhood, eventually marrying men with successful careers in the United States, and traveling around the world while living in diaspora, Jaffrey became a transnational subject rather than following an older immigration pattern that permanently cut off all ties to the immigrant's country of origin. In appealing explicitly to an American readership though the hybrid genre of the food memoir with recipes, she invokes a vision of India and the United States as former British colonies, freed from the stranglehold of imperialism, aristocracy, and class as well. Through her knowledge of regional specialties and spicy dishes, Jaffrey set out to conquer (and educate) her readers' democratic and multicultural palates with piquant tales of coming of age in the kitchen done the American way—long distance, and through trial and error.

Personal misfortune—the loss of her job as a fashion reporter and her parents' divorce—gave Tan the impetus to engage upon the culinary education she had disdained as a child and young woman. Well educated and married to a man who could afford to support them both, Tan relied on her business acumen to negotiate an advance contract for the book that became *A Tiger in the Kitchen*, a memoir with recipes about her experience of returning to Singapore to reclaim her gastronomic heritage. Tan enjoyed the opportunity to spend time with both her parents as an adult, but whereas Clarke ends *Pig Tails 'n Breadfruit* with an account of himself cooking in his mother's kitchen in a neutral middle space, neither their native Barbados nor his adopted Toronto but New Jersey, the site of her retirement, Tan's writing reclaims a place at the kitchen of her childhood home to learn from her extended family. In this measured and purposeful way, Tan embarks upon a genealogical journey of self-understanding through food, a process not entirely dissimilar to Clarke's first taste of "privilege" and Jaffrey's recipe correspondence with her mother.

Of the three writers discussed in this chapter, Cheryl Lu-Lien Tan is the most globally networked because she takes her personal quest to become an adept home cook beyond the transnational search for heritage food recipes. When she first got the hankering to prepare homemade versions of Singaporean food, Tan instinctively turned to websites and online cooking tutorials for recipes and cooking tips. Even when not visiting family in Singapore and learning to make the dishes of her childhood, Tan also actively participated in online chat rooms and cooking challenges. Tan's engagement in global, virtual cooking communities organized around a shared love of trying new things and expanding their existing skill set mark her as distinctly influenced by, and conversant in, the social media universe that characterizes this era. Thus, her nostalgic quest for her family's traditional foods is part and parcel of her larger interest in mastering the art of cooking, not merely a way to present herself as a respectable exotic. Tan's love of cooking helped her find peers scattered across the globe who view cooking as a way to pursue lifelong learning. Even cooks who never prepare the dishes of specific recipes they read may nonetheless take away useful knowledge from the mere act of having read them. Written recipes lend themselves to trial and error: baking is a less forgiving style of food preparation than is sautéing, for example, but one can always try again and seek to have better results the next time. Cooking techniques, once mastered, may be customized to suit the availability of certain ingredients in one's pantry. Recipes also serve as reference sources, indicating which flavor profiles are known to be complementary.

By casting herself in the role of a kitchen amateur—not someone wholly ignorant of the first principles of cooking, but rather a person with a newfound interest in mastering the many challenges of the kitchen, Tan acknowledges that the lure of knowledge for its own sake can be hard to resist. However, *A Tiger in the Kitchen* redefines the notion of how "scholarship" girls and boys can apply the skills developed in the classroom toward new and more enriching domestic pursuits, such as cooking. Even in this context, however, Tan does not portray her gastronomic experiments as uniformly successful. Like Jaffrey, she avoids promulgating "model minority myth" surrounding Asian Americans, and therefore she is certain to convey her spectacular failures alongside her triumphs. While the cooking "tests" or "challenges" in which she participated were self-imposed, rather than part of any institutional curriculum or familial duty, she did not hide from recalling mishaps like almost burning down the kitchen while making bread during an internet baking challenge. Tan's inclusive gesture also points to the rise of network diasporic consciousness facilitated by social media, which fosters the spontaneous formation of virtual communities based on shared interests, rather than a common birthplace, ethnicity, or language.

Clarke, Jaffrey, and Tan all maintain a complex emotional relationship to both their respective birthplaces and adopted homelands. Unlike earlier generations of immigrants, or those from less affluent backgrounds, the academic and/or professional success of this group of immigrants obviates the need to assimilate entirely to mainstream culture by giving up the cultural capital they have accrued through their upbringing and education. Acting as cultural ambassadors who introduce their new compatriots to the customs and recipes that make up their respective patrimonies, these three Commonwealth immigrant food writers explicitly avoid using the culinary metaphors that dominate discussions of assimilation: they do not want their inherited foodways to be diluted by being thrown into an assimilationist "melting pot" or being tossed around in some sort of multicultural "salad bowl."[3] Instead, Clarke, Jaffrey, and Tan view their contribution to American food writing as broadening their readers' understanding of what makes up the global foodscape by contextualizing the cuisine of their birthplace with a sense of what home life in those countries was like during their childhood. Their texts also highlight those enduring elements that distinguish Barbadian, Singaporean, or Indian dishes as cultural artifacts from others around the world.

These writers regard their familiarity with non-Western languages, religions, music, art, or foodways as cultural gifts they can share with their American reading audiences. Their mastery of their respective traditional national cuisine allows the writers to remain emotionally and physically connected to the homelands they left behind when they moved to the United States to start a new life. Sharing these recipes with their American readers facilitates a virtual exchange through which the immigrant writers "give back" a cultural gift to the country that welcomed them in, even though the memoirists themselves do not abandon their transnational networks. Their textual contributions to America's increasingly sophisticated food scene reflect the changing landscape of the global food system; Clarke, Jaffrey, and Tan view and promote their own national cuisines as members of a global family of foodways we can all encounter. Whether read for entertainment, for edification, or as handy guides to help one find one's way around the kitchen, *Pig Tails 'n Breadfruit*, *Climbing the Mango Trees*, and *A*

---

3. These two culinary metaphors have been used to describe alternative processes of assimilation to the dominant white, Anglo-Saxon, Protestant culture of the United States. Food historian Donna R. Gabaccia explains the multicultural connotations of the metaphor "salad bowl, where each ingredient retains its own distinct appearance and taste" (1998, 227). The older concept of "the melting pot" can be traced back to the play by British Jewish immigrant Israel Zangwill, *The Melting Pot*.

Tiger in the Kitchen breathe new life into the tired genre of the "immigrant memoir," not only by adding the flavor of international cuisines, but also by reimagining what it means to be both an "immigrant" and an "American" in the age of internet connectivity and easy access to relatively affordable travel.

Chapter 2

Eating in Public
AS PERFORMANCE OF ASSIMILATION, DIASPORA, OR ETHNIC BELONGING

Where the first chapter followed the narrative arc of how "scholarship" boys and girls learned how to cook like their mothers and then passed down those skills virtually to their readers via their memoirs, this chapter contrasts two key circumstances where immigrants' children have to eat and be judged by their eating in public: the school cafeteria and the banquet meal that culminates a heritage tourism experience. Such judgments take place through the process I call "gastronomic surveillance," which refers to the observation and policing of a person's eating habits to ensure conformity with an assumed norm, whether by parents or by peer groups. On the one hand, the narrators constantly emphasize their awareness that their schoolmates find their respective families' culinary traditions to be strange and out of keeping with what everyone else eats. On the other hand, the narrators' parents, who accompany them on their visits to their ancestral homeland, turn their "American" children's consumption of traditional foods into a spectacle that proves they did not repudiate their cultural identity when they immigrated. This chapter explores how the conflict between nativist peer pressure to assimilate to mainstream American foodways and parental expectations that kids partake of their family's heritage cuisine without complaint lead writers to develop either an ethnic or a diasporic framework through which to qualify their own sense of belonging to the United States.

Linda Furiya's *Bento Box in the Heartland: My Japanese Girlhood in Whitebread America*, Leslie Li's *Daughter of Heaven: A Memoir with Earthly Recipes*, Diana Abu-Jaber's *The Language of Baklava*, and Colette Rossant's *Apricots on the Nile* and *Return to Paris* detail multiple border-crossings that are literal, such as when some of the writers spend a portion of their formative years living abroad in their familial compounds in Japan, Jordan, mainland China, or Egypt, as well as figurative, like the daily intersections of the private sphere of the household and the public world of the writers' school lives as children eating in the cafeteria. As immigrants' daughters, Furiya, Li, Abu-Jaber, and Rossant discuss the complexities inherent in assimilating to mainstream culture while also cultivating their knowledge about their ethnic roots and cultural heritage. They also demonstrate their appreciation of their parents' or grandparents' experience of immigration—and the limits of their own half-immigrant experience—through heritage tourism, by traveling to the ancestral homeland in the company of a parent who serves as a native guide and informant.

These memoirs suggest that eating in public, whether at the school cafeteria or in a restaurant setting, constitutes a performance of the writers' or their families' culinary citizenship that is subject to the approval of others: what they eat marks them as either fellow "Americans" or as "foreign" members of the culture the immigrants left behind. By portraying "culinary citizenship" as a negotiated status that must be somehow approved by one's compatriots, these memoirs distinguish it as an identity category separate from the self-chosen membership in a diasporic or ethnic community, which primarily entails an individual's conscious decision to maintain ties with the culture of the ancestral homeland. Geographic proximity to other immigrant families is not a requirement but can strengthen diasporic or ethnic ties, whereas assimilation to mainstream American culture is socially expected of immigrants and their families and often policed by individual citizens who, unasked, remind naturalized citizens to "act (and eat) American" or "go home." Living without the social safety net of an ethnic enclave community, public eating becomes the way through which immigrant families negotiate their Otherness, the parents as immigrants and their children as half-immigrants, to the dominant culture of the community where they reside.

By emphasizing how their families exemplify the difficulties inherent in adapting and assimilating to American culture and outlining how the next generation negotiates the fine line between their inherited half-immigrant status and their emerging ethnic or diasporic consciousness, *Bento Box in the Heartland, Daughter of Heaven, The Language of Baklava, Apricots on the Nile,* and *Return to Paris* help their audiences develop a more nuanced understanding of what is at stake in the process of national identity formation. In this chapter, I read the performances of national identity that take place both within the immigrant household as well as out in public as social constructs whose boundaries and expectations are in a state of continual negotiation. Historian Knut Oyangen puts this in perspective when he reminds us that regardless of how private we assume food preparation and consumption are, these acts actually take place against the backdrop of trade on a global scale:

> Due to the sheer complexity of any food system—including the availability of foodstuffs, the proper equipment and skills needed to prepare food "correctly," and the accepted circumstances of eating—immigrants had to adapt or adjust in some way to new culinary realities. Since food habits have meaning only in relation to a sociocultural totality, preparing and consuming the same foods in a new context is as much an act of innovation, assertion, and transformation as it is an act of reproducing tradition. Indeed, what passed for the unconscious reproduction of tradition was often a conscious performance of identity. To examine individual immigrants' perceptions, conceptions, and emotional responses to food and food-related events that collided with prior experience and preconceived notions is therefore an integral part of analyzing immigrants' adaptive behavior. (Oyangen 2009, 324)

Oyangen cautions against an easy dismissal of the immigrant parents' desire to eat familiar foods with their family as outward signs of retrograde nostalgia for the old country. Instead, his comments highlight that one of the challenges of immigrant life is the constant encounter with the new or the uncanny. A wholesale change of alimentary habits is not only unnecessary, but entirely artificial and stressful. The only parallel for this radical overhaul of one's daily diet in American society might be the experience of going away to college or to basic training, when students or service members suddenly transition from eating the meals prepared in their households to selecting from the institutional food offerings available in dining halls across campuses or military bases.

By sharing their families' immigration stories and recipes with their readers, Furiya, Li, Abu-Jaber, and Rossant serve as mediators or cultural translators, explaining or decoding the foreign world of their immigrant domestic lives for their American readers. When these memoirists travel to the land their parents left behind, they not only face a geographical disorientation parallel to what their elders experienced when they initially immigrated, but they also find that the totality of their American citizenship has been projected upon them as a marker of difference, regardless of how problematic their claim to this identity might still be Stateside. These memoirs invoke the memorable meals of their writers' pasts as a means through which to convey to their presumably American readership the idea that national identity is not immutably fixed but, rather, continually constructed, depending on the situation.

School Lunches: Conflict in the Cafeteria

Eating is the most intimate personal activity that is routinely performed in public. Roland Barthes discusses the relative importance of public eating in Western society in the context of his reading of Jean Anthelme Brillat-Savarin's *The Physiology of Taste* (1825): "Doubtless, a general ethnology could really show that eating is in all places and at all times a social act. We eat together, that is the universal law. This alimentary sociality can assume many forms, many alibis, many nuances, according to societies, according to periods" (Barthes 1989, 267). As a normative process, with parents and caregivers monitoring food consumption and inculcating good manners by introducing the basic tenets of etiquette and politeness, eating is also one of the first and most concrete ways through which children become acculturated to society. Conflicts ensue when children fail to exhibit proper eating behavior at the table—whether through a refusal to partake at all of the food served to them or by consuming either too much or not enough of a given dish or meal. It is perhaps a universal fact that frazzled parents resort to discipline in order to enforce the basic gastronomic rules of their household.

In the United States, school-age children do not consume all of their meals at home, but must negotiate a new social arena when eating lunch in a common public setting: the school cafeteria or lunchroom. Donna Gabaccia explains that during the nineteenth century, home economists instituted culinary assimilation programs throughout large cities in the United States in an effort to assimilate both Native Americans and immigrants into the national fabric of society, especially as the frontier kept moving westward. Gabaccia refers to this process as "culinary Americanization" (Gabaccia 1998, 130) and points out that it was not always imposed from above, but sometimes requested by immigrant groups themselves. As a performance of assimilation to mainstream culture, Gabaccia's "culinary Americanization" can be read as a constituent part of Mannur's "culinary citizenship" paradigm, one that privileges one experience of citizenship (assimilation) at the cost of all others.

By the late twentieth century, such formal social programs had ceased operation in public schools across the United States. The school lunchroom, however, remained a major testing ground where child members of the majority ethnic group reject or question the half-immigrants' claims to an American cultural identity primarily because of the food these youngsters consume in this public space. When eating outside of the domestic sphere, children and young adults also use the table as the arena through which to mediate their social interactions. While the school itself is a regulatory entity that promotes the observance of specific approved behaviors regarding order, noise level, and proper disposal of discarded items, each child also brings his or her own internalized sense of peer policing and control, or gastronomic surveillance, into the collective negotiations that establish the social hierarchies of the lunchroom table. In this context, propriety has less to do with the act of ingestion than with the collective judgment regarding the suitability of the lunch items being consumed: there is an informal enforcement of "culinary Americanization" that promotes the consumption of bland, odorless, processed, or standard American fare among schoolmates. The school cafeteria, thus, becomes the arena where a young child's performance of an acceptable social and racial/ethnic identity through eating can succeed or fail, creating a ripple effect that reaches into the classroom walls and beyond.

One easy way to fit in with everyone else at lunchtime is to purchase prepared meals from the cafeteria. However, most of these memoirists choose to bring in sack lunches from home instead. My school-age children assure me that gone are the days when students brought peanut butter sandwiches or leftover casseroles to eat. Even the most "all-American" children now bring seaweed wraps and kombucha for lunch, as well as Americanized international cuisine like Chinese take-out or burritos, thus freeing half-immigrant children from judgment. Back when Linda Furiya, Leslie Li, and Diana Abu-Jaber were in school, however, the national palate was far less tolerant of variety. Though they were American-born children of immigrant families, as young students these writers fully experienced the frustration and contradictions of being half-immigrants: the "foreign" food they brought to eat in the cafeteria made them susceptible to racist comments and downright ostracism due to its smelliness or other unappealing qualities. Each of them describes a key moment when the contents of her lunch box thwarted her performance of "culinary Americanization." Although all three were members of an identifiable ethnic minority within their predominantly white, Anglo elementary schools in New York (Furiya and Abu-Jaber) or Indiana (Li), Abu-Jaber enlisted the support of a larger coalition of fellow half-immigrants from different parts of the world to resist the jeers and taunting from her disapproving white American peers, whereas Li and Furiya suffered through this abuse as the sole representatives of racial and culinary Otherness in their school communities.

Linda Furiya's Japanese family was one of the very few members of an ethnic or racial minority in the small rural community of Versailles, Indiana, while she was growing up. As a preschooler, Linda had eaten lunch at home with her mother and father, who worked the second shift at an auto plant. Once she began attending school, Linda followed her older brothers' example and ate the hot lunch served at the cafeteria. Before long, she decided institutional food was much too unappetizing, so she asked her mother to pack her lunch from home. To her shock and surprise, Linda realized that her Japanese mother did not intuitively grasp the implicit social rules of the lunch room (gastronomic surveillance) that enforce "culinary Americanization" in this public space: "I unlocked my lunch box and casually peeked under the lid. My stomach lurched. I expected a classic elementary school lunch of a bologna, cheese and Miracle Whip sandwich and a bag of Durkee's potato sticks, but all I saw were three round rice balls wrapped in waxed paper" (Furiya 2006, 5). Being confronted by the physical reminder of the differences between her social milieu in American public school and her mother's Japanese domestic world made the young girl feel ashamed and embarrassed. Reclaiming the adult narrator persona, Furiya then confesses that even as a girl, she could neither wholly disown her heritage by throwing the Japanese food away, nor bravely embrace it by eating the rice balls in front of everyone. The compromise solution she devised to this dilemma highlights her in-between status as a half-immigrant: Linda performed her "culinary Americanization" by eating only the fruit and desserts included in her lunch box while in the company of her peers, but she successfully evaded their pernicious gastronomic surveillance by hiding the Japanese food like rice balls in her pockets to eat alone later in the school lavatory. The chapter ends with a recipe for rice balls in four flavors, thereby conveying that the adult Furiya does not feel judged by her readers for her ethnic food heritage but instead celebrates it openly with an audience of likely supporters.

Writing with the distance of hindsight, the adult Furiya recalls the pain and insecurity she felt as a child, even as she now has found the pride and confidence to not only eat Japanese food openly, but also to discuss the joys and sorrows of having grown up as a lonely Japanese American

Midwesterner in *Bento Box in the Heartland*: "My desire to emulate my classmates was palpable. My *obento* lunches were a glaring reminder of the ethnic differences between my peers and me" (Furiya 2006, 5). Furiya's recollection of wanting to "emulate" the eating behavior of the same peers for whom her Japanese lunches were "glaring reminders of the ethnic differences" that separated them establishes that the system of gastronomic surveillance is not premised upon the notion of critiquing the quality of the foods it deems unacceptable; it only monitors compliance with its norms. Ironically, those very same outward markers of "the ethnic differences" are what make her family's Japanese cuisine appealing to her readers in comparison to the standard fare consumed by those she calls "Whitebread America" in the subtitle of the memoir. Thus she strategically ends all the chapters with recipes for the food her peers rejected as too "exotic" during her childhood.

Whereas Linda Furiya grew up eating traditional Japanese fare until she began attending school, Leslie Li's Chinese American mother, Genevieve, worked long hours as a fashion buyer at Macy's and thus routinely prepared an assortment of quick and convenient Western dishes like noodles in cream sauce and fish sticks for dinner when she got home. Once the girls' paternal Chinese grandmother moved in with the family after an eight-year-long wait for a visa, the traditional Chinese dishes the girls had enjoyed during a brief time spent with relatives in mainland China before the Communist takeover again graced the Li family's table. The children generally reacted well to the dietary change at home, but they balked when it came to school lunches, as Leslie recalls:

> [Grandmother's] arrival and my mother's abdication of the kitchen were evident in the lunches my sisters and I carried to school, which elicited curiosity and interest, some of it horrified. That is to say that, even though we tried to imitate our peers and sometimes had in our lunches the chemical additives we so admired in theirs, this follow-the-leaderism soon stopped. Instead of the Sno Balls and Twinkies from the local Shopwell or Grand Union, our desserts often came from faraway Chinatown. (Li 2005, 11)

This vignette opens the chapter entitled "Food Shame and Sand-Wishes," and through it Li recalls her childish belief that her peers' sugary lunchtime indulgences were indicative of similar junk-food diets at home. What the now-adult Li perceives as the end of her childish "follow-the-leaderism" was merely the result of her grandmother's reclamation of the normative parental role with regard to the family's traditional foodways.

At this early point in the family's transition from the nuclear structure led by two working parents back to the extended family life anchored by the grandmother as matriarch, the seventh grader felt as if the food in her lunch sack suddenly marked her as an outsider, a foreigner, in a way she had not necessarily stood out before, despite being one of the few non-white children at her school. Rather than cave in to the negative reaction that some of the meals she brought occasioned in the lunchroom, Leslie defied her peers' gastronomic surveillance and rejected her former "culinary Americanization" by both embracing her exotic lunches and publicly enjoying them. Her gastronomic defiance in the parochial school cafeteria is an example of her own performance of "respectable exoticism," as discussed in the previous chapter. By eating Chinese food, the girl forced her peers to acknowledge they saw her as an ethnic Outsider, as not quite as American as they saw themselves. In an inclusive gesture similar to Furiya's in *Bento Box*, Li concludes the chapter with a recipe for beef and tomatoes in oyster sauce, which affirms Li's adult perception of her readers as more adventurous eaters than the schoolmates of her youth.

Although young Diana Abu-Jaber also experienced some of the same feelings of isolation and discrimination that Linda Furiya and Leslie Li faced, she had a larger network of potential allies in her neighborhood than either of the other young women did. Though the Abu-Jabers were the only Arab American family in their upstate New York neighborhood, they were far from being the only immigrants. *The Language of Baklava* discusses two instances of public eating in which Arab cuisines and customs occasioned diametrically opposed reactions. The first took place in the front yard of the Abu-Jaber family home in Syracuse and featured an anti-assimilationist immigrant coalition in her neighborhood. One early spring day, soon after the Abu-Jabers returned to the United States after a two-year sojourn in Jordan, the family enjoyed an outdoor picnic in their front yard of their home. Seeing the smoke from Bud's grill, the neighbors engaged in their own version of gastronomic surveillance when they came over to investigate what was going on. On the bus ride to school the next day, one of Diana's schoolmates informed her that eating in the front yard was unacceptable, meaning un-American:

> "Well, you know, of course. My parents saw you out there the other night. I heard them talking with the neighbors. They said it was an 'unholy disgrace.' See, okay, the thing is, you better know that in this country nobody eats in the front yard. Really. Nobody." She looks at me solemnly and sadly, her bangs a perfect cylinder above her brows. "If your family doesn't know

how to behave, my parents will have to find out about getting you out of this neighborhood." (Abu-Jaber 2005, 82)

Abu-Jaber's interlocutor was conveying her own parents' attempts to engage in "culinary Americanization" by articulating what people "in this country" do and do not do as the unquestioned norm that needs to be followed by all immigrants. The traumatized young Diana told her neighbor, an older immigrant from Italy, about the hurtful comments on the bus, and the woman decided to strike back by staging another, much larger front-yard picnic, this time involving multiple immigrant families. She explicitly made a point to invite the Anglo American neighbors to come sample the international food on offer at this public neighborhood gathering. This is yet another way through which this memoir validates interethnic solidarity as a tool to combat feelings of isolation or inferiority caused by being the only members of a distinctly recognizable ethnic or immigrant minority within a dominant society. Luckily, both the recipes for Bud's grilled chicken, humorously titled "'Distract the Neighbors' Grilled Chicken" and described as a "delightful, simple dish that will fill the neighborhood with a gorgeous scent" (Abu-Jaber 2005, 79), are included in the volume.

While this defiant action quelled any subsequent overt criticism, Abu-Jaber recounts this episode in order to track its ripple effect in her own cafeteria eating life later. The second incident is emblematic of Diana's gastronomic rebellion, which resonates more with Leslie Li's experience of defiant consumption of her Chinese lunches than with Linda Furiya's furtive eating habits in elementary school. Simply put, schoolmates in the cafeteria always found the food Diana Abu-Jaber brought for lunch to be not only interesting in its odd combination of aromas and appearance, but also tasty. In elementary school, Diana recalls that the appeal of her school lunches broke up a friendship between two little girls she knew, simply because one of them expressed interest in trying the foreign food while the other did not dare: "Jamie Faraday used to be best friends with Sally Holmes until I appeared in the lunchroom with my bags full of cold roasted chicken kabobs slathered in hummus and wrapped in pita bread" (Abu-Jaber 2005, 77). Thus, although the cultural practice of eating outside earns her family public reproach from their neighbors, the children who eat lunch with Diana at school actually perceive her Arab food as delicious and, therefore, desirable. Gastronomic surveillance is at work in the cafeteria as much as in the neighborhood, but the adults are more likely to demand and enforce "culinary Americanization" in terms of eating etiquette than the children are in terms of the flavors of the foods they will accept.

Though Colette Rossant spent her childhood outside of the United States (in her father's family compound in Egypt), she also mentions experiences of gastronomic surveillance at school similar to those Furiya, Li, and Abu-Jaber underwent. The first two volumes of Rossant's memoirs, *Apricots on the Nile* and *Return to Paris,* attest to young Colette's emotionally fraught relationships with her mother and maternal grandmother, neither of whom taught her to cook. Each of the memoirs includes at least one vignette in which the older relative uses the public consumption of food as an opportunity to insult or dismiss Rossant's taste or cooking ability. Colette spent the Second World War living in Egypt with her father's family. Upon her return to Paris after the war, Colette's grandmother shamed the plump teenager into dropping her "Egyptian" weight to better conform to the slim beauty standards of postwar France. Thus, it was her grandmother, rather than her peers, who most overtly subjected the child to gastronomic surveillance and "culinary Frenchification" (rather than Americanization) by constantly referring to her half-immigrant status as the mixed-race daughter of a French woman and an Egyptian man as shameful in its hybridity.

One particularly galling scene of her grandmother's harsh lesson in acculturation takes place at a restaurant, when she criticized Colette's meal choices as either too Egyptian or not French enough: "If I suggested the fish of the day or berries with cream, my grandmother would say in a pinched voice, 'Cet enfant n'a aucun gout. Elle est vraiment une Egyptienne!' (This child has no taste. She really is an Egyptian!)" (Rossant 2004b, 66; translation in original). By virtue of taking place in a restaurant rather than behind closed doors at home, this public confrontation demonstrates Rossant's fiscal and filial dependence upon her grandmother, who thus had the power and influence to force her granddaughter to engage in more "acceptable" performances of gender and national identity through food. Ironically, Colette later found public validation for her good taste as a teenager when she chanced upon Café Laure, a food establishment near the school whose house specialty was an enticing ham sandwich (*sandwich au jambon*), "filled with a light *pistou,* a dark green sauce made with parsley and herbs, redolent of garlic" (Rossant 2004b, 74). Once word got out, "half the lycee learned of our discovery, and Mme Laure's café was full all day." Like Abu-Jaber found out in her own school, garlicky food can be the key to social success in certain circles. Rossant's appetite for spicy food, once scorned by her grandmother, became the very means through which Colette overcame her outsider status within the school community, even if she was never quite accepted as fully French by her peers. Sadly, the chapter does not include the recipe for this delicious ham sandwich. This episode marks a turning point in the young Colette's self-esteem; from here on out, she began thinking of herself as a denizen of the city of Paris instead of a citizen of either France or Egypt: "I was no longer 'l'Egyptienne'; I was 'la Parisienne,' with an attitude" (Rossant 2004b, 78). Ironically, it is at this point in her development that Colette Rossant met the young American man she eventually married, and with whom she would once again leave the country of her birth.

The institutionalized surveillance of an environment such as the school cafeteria promotes the normativity of assimilation through the overt policing of what (and how much) people eat. Students and coworkers monitor one another's lunches, searching for clues to culinary noncompliance. While a refined palate can sometimes turn the tables and render alluring the exotic and spicy meals eaten by half-immigrants like Leslie Li, Diana Abu-Jaber, and Colette Rossant, the collective will to blandness of younger children like Linda Furiya's schoolmates is strong enough to squelch any ambivalent claim to ethnic difference. The fastest way to fit in and assimilate into the dominant culture of the school or the nation is by eating what everyone else does, even if one then supplements it by sneaking extra food.

Double Consciousness and Ethnic Awakening

Furiya, Li, and Abu-Jaber recount particular moments in their childhoods when they each experienced double consciousness: as young girls, Linda, Leslie, and Diana were painfully aware of the differences between how they were perceived by others (as immigrants/outsiders like their families) and how they saw themselves (as Americans).[1] Diana Abu-Jaber's fair skin allowed her to physically assimilate into mainstream American culture to a degree that was not available to Leslie or Linda, whose physical features marked them as racially Other.

Moving to the Bay Area and witnessing the variety and diversity of Asian American culture made Furiya and Li appreciate their specific ethnic heritage and half-immigrant experience more than they had when they were

---

1. There is no consensus within Asian American studies scholarship as to whether or not it is possible to experience "double consciousness" akin to how W. E. B. Du Bois described it in *The Souls of Black Folk*. Eric Liu rejects the premise of self-alienation experienced by minorities, citing it as "a central tenet of multicultural ideology" (Liu 1996). Liu argues that since race is a construct, rather than a biological fact, ethnicity and nationality are constructs too, and thus neither whiteness nor American-ness as ideals should be presumed to be monolithic.

growing up as part of the only Asian American family in their respective small communities. Leslie Li and Linda Furiya write as women who have experienced an ethnic awakening and made a point of claiming an "Asian American" identity as adults for both political and emotional reasons. In *Immigrant Acts: On Asian American Cultural Politics*, Lisa Lowe points out that the term "Asian American" can be applied to Asian-born immigrants to the United States as a rhetorical category that functions as a marker of ethnicity: "the majority of Asian Americans are at present Asian-born rather than multiple-generation" (Lowe 1996, 7). Thus, using this umbrella term as a marker of ethnic identity as a matter of course does not force a person to embrace or reject immigration as a part of his or her experience in America. This identity category was not available to them as children, as Furiya explains in the context of her own experience:

> Growing up Japanese American in a rural farm town was saturated with emotions that made me feel as if I didn't truly belong and that I was on the outside looking in.
>
> I felt suspended between two worlds I didn't belong in—the American culture where I spent my entire girlhood and the Japanese culture that matched my physical features but not my upbringing. (Furiya 2006, 300)

Written after this epiphany, *Bento Box in the Heartland* chronicles Furiya's transformation from double outsider—too Americanized for her family, too Japanese for dominant society—into a member of a larger, identifiable group of people with similar backgrounds but not delimited by nationality or ethnicity alone.

Like Furiya, Li finds comfort in the very broadness of the term "Asian American" as a political marker of belonging, looking to food to establish common ground between all the various groups included under that rubric. Leslie's celebration of the Asian American journal *Rice* for its strategic deployment of culinary normativity (rather than Americanization) helps her take pride in her Chinese American upbringing as symbolic of a larger experience of being ethnic American:

> Rice is common fare among Asian-Americans—perhaps the one across-the-board common denominator that we of Asian extraction share. Other than rice, what do we have in common? Certainly not religion. We're either Hindu, Muslim, Buddhist, or Christian by conversion. Physical features? A Chinese-American will hardly be mistaken for an Indian-American, or a Filipino-American for a Japanese-American. And our secular customs

and political systems differentiate us further still. But we all eat, much and often rice. (Li 2005, 82)

Although both Li and Furiya cook and use recipes to punctuate the anecdotes from their lives about which they write, only Leslie Li conflates the performance of eating a staple of "Asian American" cuisine with the fact of being an Asian American.[2]

In contrast, Diana Abu-Jaber's experience as an immigrant's daughter was complicated by her parents' mixed-race marriage: her father, Gus, was Jordanian, whereas her mother was an American woman of Irish-German ancestry. The family's Arab exoticism was sometimes fetishized and other times the cause of stigma in their hometown of Syracuse, New York. Abu-Jaber writes that by the time she was six years old, she had already figured out that her family regularly performed different cultural identities depending on whether they inhabited the domestic sphere or went out in public: "I learn early: We are Arab at home and American in the streets" (Abu-Jaber 2005, 5). In this usage, both "Arab" and "American" are floating signifiers that include Diana's American mother, alongside her immigrant husband and their Arab American children. By embracing their dual identity, the family stands together as a unit rather than being divided by nationality; they are all half-immigrants, since Gus's immigration journey affects how they are all perceived. While she publicly claims a shared ethnicity with her father as Arab Americans once she embarked upon a career as a novelist, she knows that in their neighbors' eyes, his immigrant status and accented speech set the whole family apart during her youth as "not quite" Americans.

Where Leslie Li and Linda Furiya found empowerment by claiming an ethnic cultural identity while living in a city with a considerable Asian American population, young Diana forged friendships with other child half-immigrants, which helped her take pride in her status as not quite a member of the dominant Anglo-American social circles in Syracuse. In an example of how such alliances work, Diana Abu-Jaber discusses how their love of food differentiates immigrant standards for physical beauty from those of mainstream Americans: "My immigrant-kid friends are not on diets. Most of us have parents from countries where a certain lushness is considered alluring in a woman. We've grown up in houses redolent with

---

2. One problem that arises with this culinary calculus, however, is that Asian Americans are not the only people who regularly eat Asian food or even rice as a staple in their diet.

the foods of other places" (Abu-Jaber 2005, 161). The evident joy these "immigrant-kid(s)" take in the food they eat irks the American girls, who resent them for not subscribing to the same restrictive beauty standard that privileges thinness over womanly curves. Abu-Jaber's embrace of other immigrant children as part of her support network as a child and teenager was strategic: while there may not have been enough families from any one place of origin to establish an ethnic enclave in Syracuse during this time, the immigrant kids could imbue their nondominant status with a collective identity forged by their shared love of spicy and aromatic foods, even as they themselves became assimilated to mainstream culture. These young people reach out to one another to establish social circles in which immigration is, if not the new normal, then at least normal enough to be a viable alternative to Anglo-American conformity.

Reclaiming Diasporic Ties

Although it was her father's terminal illness, rather than the beginning of World War II, that prompted Rossant's family to relocate to Egypt when she was six years old, the conflict in Europe did prolong her stay well beyond the period of his illness and death. As a result, young Colette was raised until the age of fifteen by her paternal grandparents, financially successful Egyptian Jewish businesspeople who employed Muslim cooks and servants, some local and others from as far away as Sudan, within the household. When she returned to Paris after the end of the war, Colette had to become acculturated to her country of origin once more. Her accent and the dark pigment of her skin bore the traces of her Egyptian sojourn, to which others, her grandmother and school peers among them, pointed with disdain. Colette found that her complex heritage and family history were seen as an asset when she immigrated to the United States following her marriage to James Rossant. She explains that "being French, however, was a distinct advantage in New York City. My Egyptian 'half' made me seem even more exotic to Americans just beginning to be interested in things foreign. For the first time in five years, I could speak openly about Cairo" (Rossant 2004a, 148). Rossant's newfound freedom to celebrate her heritage was made possible by a combination of factors: Americans' renewed engagement in world affairs after the conclusion of World War II, the fact that many GIs had spent time in France and had fond memories of French food, and Rossant's move to New York City, arguably the most cosmopolitan of all American cities.

Heritage Tourism and Celebratory Banquets

Just as the scenes of public eating discussed above encapsulate a period in their lives when the memoirists had to eat whatever their parents packed for them, this next section focuses on instances in these women's adult lives when they relive a similar degree of disempowerment by traveling with their immigrant parents to the family's ancestral homeland. Linda Furiya, Leslie Li, and Diana Abu-Jaber embark upon heritage tourism both to learn more about their roots and also to experience a different family dynamic than the one in which they grew up. By returning to their birthplace, the immigrant parents demonstrate their membership in a diaspora community with ongoing intellectual, emotional, and perhaps even economic connections to the country of origin. At the same time, the immigrants' children confront and test the limits of their own American half-immigrant identity, but they do so collectively, through the lens of the family unit. Now, however, the power dynamics are reversed. Whereas in America the immigrant parents had to rely upon their U. S.-born children to navigate American customs and social situations, in their countries of origin they now assume the role of mediators between their daughters and the local customs and language.

Although the phenomena of family heritage tourism has not drawn much critical attention so far, postcolonial scholars like Fazila Bhimji have already noted the tendency of second-generation ethnic subjects—the same group of people I refer to as "half-immigrants"—to participate in this tourist economy. Within the specific context of British Muslim women, Bhimji observes: "With increased global connections, children of immigrants are more likely than ever to visit their parents' homeland where they may feel both an insider and outsider to the particular culture" (Bhimji 2008, 414). She suggests that there may be certain spaces within the immigrant parents' country, such as relatives' homes, which the second-generation traveler may feel more comfortable in or recognize as more familiar than other public spaces, but Bhimji interprets her interview subjects' experiences as evidence of their aspirations of cosmopolitanism. Asian American studies scholar Andrea Louie offers a contrasting interpretation of immigrant children's trips to their parents' homelands. She views such journeys as overdetermined exercises in personal meaning-making, especially since kinship structures lend an emotional significance to any activity the traveler undertakes in this space.

> Given their personal connections to the places which they visit, participants in this type of ethnic tourism usually desire to go beyond tourist

observations to search for more authentic and personally fulfilling experiences. In each of these cases of cultural tourism, travel abroad to one's ancestral land is done with the hope of completing part of one's identity as a hyphenated American. Thus, participants' motivations for joining these tours, the frameworks within which they interpret their experiences, and the structure of the tours themselves are shaped by the participants' experiences in the United States. (Louie 2003, 741)

I agree with Louie's and Bhimji's views that having direct kinship ties changes the context in which heritage tourists relate to their environment. Both scholars also note that among the motivating factors influencing half-immigrants to undertake such journeys is the desire to fully confront the culture of their family heritage as a way of fully grasping their own sense of American-ness or belonging. What makes the "return" journey so unusual a motif in the case of *Bento Box in the Heartland, Daughter of Heaven, The Language of Baklava, Return to Paris,* and *Apricots on the Nile* is precisely that these visits privilege two food-related sites: the first is the family kitchen and the second is a dining room, whether at the heart of the home or in public, at a banquet hall. More often than not, the trips the memoirists take with their parents involve visits with an extended family that also includes loyal servants and cooks, something different from the typical American celebration of the self-sufficient nuclear family unit. Traveling together affirms the parents' and daughters' communal sense of belonging to a transnational diasporic community more than to either the homeland or to the United States.

Eating traditional meals together during their trip helps cement the familial and national bonds between the two generations, much as it did in the United States. By traveling with their parents, Furiya, Li, Abu-Jaber, and Rossant experience firsthand some of the same disorientation, frustration, and apprehension that their elders must have felt when arriving in their respective adopted countries. While this empathy is mitigated by the temporary nature of their visits to Japan, China, Jordan, or Egypt, as the case may be, these transnational episodes in the memoirs illustrate that immigrant parents and their adult offspring can choose to bond over their shared love of both the ancestral and the adopted homelands without necessarily having equivalent claims to linguistic mastery or cultural authenticity.

When discussing the trips they take with their parents, Linda Furiya, Leslie Li, Diana Abu-Jaber, and Colette Rossant write most clearly from within the subject position of "daughter" rather than as independent writers recalling their individual pasts. These women cede their narrative authority to their parents, who use their expert knowledge of the language, customs, geography, and cuisine of their respective home countries to guide their offspring through an alternate domestic landscape. The memoirists' self-disclosures of the cultural gaffes they commit, the confusion they feel, and their inability to understand what transpires between their parents, relatives, and members of the extended family lend an air of transparency to their food memoirs with recipes, making them at once more believable and sympathetic to the readers.

Linda Furiya and Colette Rossant travel with their immigrant parents only when they are children; however, these journeys have a deep and lasting impact upon their still-forming consciousness. As young girls, Linda Furiya and Colette Rossant mastered the basics of their immigrant parents' native language. Thus, Furiya's trip to accompany her mother to Japan was a reward: by taking Linda, her parents acknowledged the child's initiative and emerging sense of ethnic pride. Furiya's family lived two hours away from the closest Japanese-language school in Cincinnati, and thus they neither required nor expected her or her brothers to take an interest in speaking or writing Japanese. As a child, Linda taught herself to read and write Japanese *hiragana* and *katakana* characters using instructional books her uncle had sent. She tested her growing mastery over the complex characters by reading her mother's grocery lists and the Japanese-language labels on food products, but it was not until she was with her relatives in Japan that she was able to appreciate how easily and fluently her mother expressed herself in her mother tongue. This trip allowed Linda to see her mother unaccented, so to speak, and gave her a new respect for the woman whom she had previously resented for depending on a child to make herself understood among her neighbors.

> "Every day after work, vendors set up stands selling all types of food outside the subway, not just yakitori," said Mom. "Some sold grilled sticky rice or fish balls. When I was your age, I bought sweet pastries before supper. I was a picky eater at that time and got away with not finishing my supper. Father never figured out that I had already eaten sweets," she said with a conspiring twinkle in her eyes. (Furiya 2006, 146)

The trip to Japan exposed young Linda to important food-related rituals, like the Japanese tea ceremony, in their proper contexts. It also, and most importantly, gave the child a glimpse into the work and family life her mother willingly relinquished in order to try her luck in an arranged marriage in the United States.

As the oldest memoirist discussed in this chapter and the only one to have lost both of her parents, Colette Rossant approaches the subject of the family's return to an ancestral homeland from multiple perspectives. The first trip she took to her father's homeland of Egypt happened when she was six years old. Given his frail state of health at the time and subsequent convalescence upon arrival, Rossant does not recall visiting the sights with him. Instead, she spent the bulk of her time in the kitchen, learning from the servants how to prepare the dishes her family enjoyed. Like Furiya, Colette demonstrates her linguistic initiative when she learns Arabic in order to communicate better with her family's servants. From them, Colette learned to enjoy traditional Egyptian fare as well as meals from her Sephardic Jewish heritage.[3] Colette's relationship to her own Judaism is complicated by her mother's decision to enroll her in a Catholic girl's school in Egypt, and her maternal grandmother's desperate strategy to ensure her own and Colette's brother's survival in occupied France by passing as a Catholic. These circumstances mean that Colette did not experience her Jewish identity in terms of its global and diasporic connections.

As an adult, Rossant returns to Egypt twice, but in a new role: that of the immigrant parent herself embarking upon heritage tourism with her children. First with her son in the seventies, and later with her daughter towards the end of the nineties, Colette Rossant set out to find the paternal compound she had told her children so much about in order to prove that her stories were indeed true. During each visit, Rossant relied on the help of locals in order to find the place, but managed to recapture a sense of belonging by visiting the outdoor markets she used to frequent as a child accompanied by her grandmother and the family's cook. Rossant sought to establish the authenticity of the stories she had passed on about her childhood by taking her children to the restaurants where she ate as a child:

> I asked the concierge if there was a restaurant called Aboushakra. "It is a chain," he answered, "but the original is not far from the hotel." We walked to the restaurant, sidestepping taxis and cars . . . Abaoushakra had not changed in fifty years. Well, not completely. What had changed was the lighting and the advertising on the wall. As we entered the restaurant, I saw an enormous charcoal oven filled with tiny squab cooking. The room was uglier than I remembered, with dirty pink walls, fluorescent lights,

---

3. In *Apricots on the Nile*, Rossant herself refers to her family as "Middle Eastern Jews" (Rossant 2004a, 32) rather than using the adjective "Sephardic," which is more commonly used in American parlance. By the time *Return to Paris*, the second volume of her memoir, was published, Rossant had switched to "Sephardic" to describe her family.

and plastic baskets filled with toasted pita on each table. We ordered squab, *tehina*, vine leaves, hummus, and tomato salad with pickles. The tasty squab were sprinkled with cumin, garlic and lime. We ate them with our fingers and laughed when we looked at our plates. Virtually no bones were left; we had chewed on everything. (Rossant 2004, 157)

This recollection of the restaurant meal with her daughter is the public performance through which Rossant truly reclaims her Egyptian heritage, an aspect of her family history about which her Jewish French grandmother had made young Colette feel ashamed. By passing her love of Egyptian food at the same eating establishment where her grandfather would take her for meals, Rossant symbolically bequeaths this cuisine down to the next generation, acting as a culinary guide, of sorts, to her half-immigrant, American-born daughter.

Like young Colette, Diana Abu-Jaber also travelled with her family to her father's homeland when she was a child, but this sojourn only lasted a year. During that time, she learned to communicate in Arabic with other children and with the family's servants, which made her American mother uneasy and somewhat resentful. Ironically, it was this time away that helped cement a strong sense of American identity in the Abu-Jaber daughters, who clamored for pancakes after spending so much time eating only Arab food. The memoir contains a touching scene of syncretic or fusion cooking within the Abu-Jaber compound, in which the family and the neighbors all chip in, bringing bread, vegetables, mint, and yogurt to make a whole meal out of what they call the "burnt American flat food" (Abu-Jaber 2005, 38), in reference to the pancakes her mother overcooked in the compound's courtyard.

Bud Abu-Jaber experienced a growing dissatisfaction with the opportunities available for him in Jordan and moved the family back to the United States. It was with great joy, however, that Diana welcomes her father's extended visit to her Jordanian apartment toward the end of the year she spent there on a Fulbright fellowship. With his arrival, the extended family dynamic Diana had been enjoying changed. No longer the favored guest, she now experienced the traditional gender roles assigned to women in Jordanian society—her domicile was now seen as belonging to her father; she had to accommodate an endless stream of family guests for lunch and dinner instead of receiving their hospitality as before; she ate after the men did. However, the time she spent watching Bud react to the modernization of his home country allowed Diana to realize she shared his Arab outlook of thinking the answer to problems lies somewhere out there rather than her American mother's more self-reliant attitude.

Of the four memoirists discussed in this study, Diana Abu-Jaber comes the closest to having a full understanding of her immigrant parent's experience of dislocation and personal exile from a beloved homeland, perhaps because as an accomplished novelist, she can project herself into her father's consciousness as if he were one of the characters in her fiction. Her grasp of Arabic will never equal his; Bud's English will always stay accented and unidiomatic, but both father and daughter experience a shared Arab sensibility that distinguishes them from their beloved American wife and mother. Thus, while both Diana and her father experienced homesickness together in Jordan, their journeys around Amman helped them reaffirm their joint sense of belonging to the Arab diaspora in the United States.

Like Diana Abu-Jaber in *The Language of Baklava*, Leslie Li travelled with her father to their ancestral homeland. However, Li's parents are divorced, which made the choice of which parent to favor at any given part of the narrative more fraught. By discussing heritage tourism primarily through the trips the writer took with her father, *Daughter of Heaven* breaks with the trend toward matrilineal narratives so popular in Asian American fiction after the success of writers like Amy Tan and Maxine Hong Kingston. I nonetheless choose to read the two trips Leslie Li takes to China with her father through the lens of American studies scholar Silvia Schultermandl's concept of "transnational matrilineage" (2009, 10), because Li puts a high value on her relationship with Nai-nai, the Chinese grandmother who cooked for her during her childhood and repatriated after the Li girls were grown. From Schultermandl's feminist perspective, transnationalism allows for Asian American (grand)daughters to achieve solidarity with their mother (figures) by reconciling with the family histories they have been bequeathed. While Schultermandl uses the term specifically to describe the tensions between first- and second-generation mother-daughter bonds in Asian American fiction, I want to broaden its scope to encompass the granddaughter-grandmother relationship (the first and third generations) in the memoir *Daughter of Heaven* precisely because Li's mother, Genevive, was Amerasian, the daughter of a European-descended American and a Chinese man, so her only experience of China and its culture was limited to the few years she lived there with her husband, before the Communist take-over.

Leslie Li underwent the same process of discovering and reclaiming her Chinese ethnic and cultural roots that Schultermandl argues other mother-daughter couples experience, but her relationship to Nai-nai was triangulated via her immigrant father. After moving to California and developing a sense of ethnic pride as a member of the Asian American community, Li decided to reconnect with the woman who raised and cooked for her and her sisters. Leslie asked her father to accompany her on two visits to see Nai-nai, acting as Leslie's guide and interpreter. During the first trip, Leslie managed to write down recipes for the dishes Nai-nai prepared for her family when she was growing up. But, due to her grandmother's advanced old age, Lesliehad to rely on the help of the younger family cook, whom Nai-nai had trained personally. This is the moment in the narrative that most clearly exemplifies "transnational matrilineage" as an empowering alliance between a Chinese grandmother and her Chinese American granddaughter, facilitated by the local servant girl and Leslie's Americanized immigrant father.

Much like Abu-Jaber's *The Language of Baklava, Daughter of Heaven* portrays father and daughter as members of a diasporic community. While the trips allowed father and daughter to reconcile and discuss private family history after a brief estrangement, their visits to Nai-nai were also public events due to the grandmother's status as a political figure: the widow of Li Zongren, who had been acting president of the Chinese Republic when the mainland came under Communist control. Thus, Li and her father's filial duty becomes manipulated by the Chinese government, who repackage and market the event as pro-heritage tourism propaganda to lure other "overseas Chinese" to return and spend American dollars. Though Leslie feels her grandmother lived her life in the shadow of her husband's fame as a military leader and politician, Nai-nai's longevity served a more sinister purpose than merely allowing her granddaughter to pay her respects. The Chinese government transformed the occasion of her centenary into a big public celebration marked by the presence of dignitaries, poets, and reporters and concluding with a lavish banquet, thereby subsuming the personal significance of the occasion to the family under the national imperative of promoting China's image as a modern country with traditional values:

> My father passed me a plate of birthday cake—a small slice of a two-layer yellow cake thickly spackled with white frosting ornamented with fluted pink-frosted ribbons and rossettes—and looked at me with anticipatory, even apprehensive eyes. He had just fed Nai-nai a forkful to the popping of flashbulbs, the click of camera lenses, the whir of camcorders. I nudged a bit of cake, complete with rosette, onto the fork which I lowered toward my grandmother. She opened her mouth, birdlike, avaricious, to receive the offering. It was the cake that was important, its taste and the pleasure it gave her that she craved. That I, her granddaughter, was at the other end of the fork was meaningless. (Li 2005, 254)

This was the last time Leslie Li and her father traveled together to learn something about their shared heritage. In this episode, the Li family was co-opted into the political performance of Nai-nai's birthday through public eating: both father and daughter show deference to their elderly relative by feeding her birthday cake. Ironically, Western-style birthday cakes have no place in traditional Chinese birthday celebrations; noodles are the usual food of choice. Thus, the frosted cake became yet another propaganda tool through which the Chinese government hoped to attract American-born Chinese heritage travelers to visit their hereditary homeland; this familiar foodstuff was meant to convey mainland China's modernity and thus downplay the cultural differences between it and the United States. This exercise in institutionalized gastronomic surveillance was an attempt to lure the diaspora "home" and profit from its nostalgia for the past.

Qualified Claim of American Belonging

Whether arranged privately or undertaken for official purposes, these memoirists' heritage visits with their parents allow both generations to contrast memory with lived reality, and the most rewarding way this happens is through eating. Sometimes the meals do not live up to expectations, but at other times the family can be nicely surprised by both the food and the warm welcome they receive. Regardless of when it takes place chronologically, the trip "home" constitutes the last step in Furiya's, Li's, Abu-Jaber's, and Rossant's process of self-definition and identity acceptance beyond their early sense of being marked by their parents' immigrant status. In other words, heritage tourism makes clear to these writers that there are definite limits to how marked they can or should be by an older relative's immigration journey. If teasing in the school cafeteria made these women feel like half-immigrants in their natal land, travel abroad confirms their sense of themselves as Americans and impels them to craft this personal sense of citizenship and belonging to communities of their own choosing.

Bento Box in the Heartland, Daughter of Heaven, The Language of Baklava, Return to Paris, and *Apricots on the Nile* all chart the writers' dual process of coming to terms with their ethnic identity while also explaining to their readers what is at stake in claiming such a subject position. Linda Furiya, Leslie Li, Diana Abu-Jaber, and Colette Rossant share both their individual recollections and favorite recipes with readers in a textual invitation to the table. By speaking as individuals rather than as representative members of ethnic enclave communities and including recipes from a variety of culinary traditions, these women promote the idea that private cooking and public eating can be both emotionally and politically fraught performances that signal one's membership in various communities. These memoirs support the notion that one's national identity is neither static nor one-dimensional, but rather has to be personally claimed and performed through activities that can include, but are not limited to, food preparation and consumption.

Chapter 3

Mapping the New South(west)ern Home

*C*hef Edward Lee is a prominent member of the increasing internal migration to the so-called New South. He moved to Kentucky from his native New York in 2003, and has come to be part of the cultural life of the state and the region. Known for his appreciation for good whiskey almost as much as for competing in season nine of *Top Chef,* Lee credits his move down South with giving him a renewed appreciation of his experience as the grandchild of Korean immigrants. In his memoir, *Smoke and Pickles: Recipes and Stories from a New Southern Kitchen,* Lee explains how he came to feel at home in the South:

> Over time, Louisville, and, by extension, the American South, embraced me as an adopted son. I was not surprised by that. It was effortless. What I didn't expect was how I would come full circle and rediscover myself as a child of Korean immigrants. That all the lovely and resourceful traditions of the Southern landscape would propel me back to the kitchen of my grandmother's spicy, garlicky foods: Soft grits remind me of congee; jerky of cuttlefish; chowchow of kimchi. My Korean forefathers' love of pickling is rivaled only by Southerners' love of pickling. BBQ, with its intricate techniques of marinades and rubs, is the backbone of both cuisines. Buttermilk has become my miso, ubiquitous and endearing. It shows up in everything

from dressings to marinades to desserts, but never in the foreground, always as a platform to let other ingredients shine. (Lee 2013, ix)

Lee embodies the new migration to the South through his professional connection to, and appreciation of, its historic foodways. He takes a syncretic approach to his cooking—using local ingredients in ways that his ancestors used their analogous Korean staples, and in so doing, he creolizes the cuisines of both traditions, creating a whole new southern cuisine. This geographic relocation made the chef more aware of his family's history of migration and, in so doing, brought the concept of kinship to the forefront, framing his understanding of his relationship to his new home as an "adopted son" of the South. Much like buttermilk, which Lee uses only to help the featured ingredients in his dishes stand out, his Korean American ethnicity is also in the background of Lee's self-proclaimed regional identity as a southerner. His professional southerner identity is affirmed through both his restaurant and his membership in the Southern Foodways Alliance (SFA). For outsiders to be "embraced" by the diverse New South and its legendary hospitality, they need to change their fundamental relationship to American-ness, learning to regard themselves as co-creators of an almost mythic geographic region with distinct cultural and culinary identities.

An academic nonprofit organization, the Southern Foodways Alliance identifies its mission as the study of "the diverse food cultures of the changing South," with the full knowledge that a celebration of the South must be done without nostalgia both "thoughtfully and oftentimes critically." The editors of the recent SFA-sponsored collection of essays, *The Larder: Food Studies Methods from the American South* (2013), present a primer on the practice of such scholarship and echo the organization's sense that the American South is a region in flux, where tradition and innovation coexist and cross-fertilize one another. Elizabeth Engelhardt's introduction proclaims: "Southern identity is now being fractured and reconceived to reflect a twenty-first century South informed by, but not wholly defined by, nineteenth- and twentieth-century racial politics. Even as we wonder whether the South coheres, southern food traditions do not appear to be imperiled" (Edge, Engelhardt, and Ownby 2013, 4). Andrew Warnes remarks in the chapter on authenticity: "On southern grounds, after all, ideas of authenticity and invention at once acquire added urgency and develop new character. In no other American region does quite so much kitsch or knowingly ersatz culture flourish in such close proximity with so many traditions that present themselves as time honored and anything but invented" (Edge, Engelhardt, and Ownby 2013, 346). Following in that spirit of inclusiveness, and fully aware that southern and southwestern states continue to welcome a steady influx of immigrants while also serving as the home base for several diasporic populations who maintain close ties to their countries of origins—Cuban, Haitian, and increasingly, Puerto Rican communities among them—this chapter endeavors to remap the two regions of the South and Southwest into a larger geocultural space marked by overlapping and complementary culinary traditions.

The memoirs examined herein discuss how experiences of travel and displacement, movement away from or into the South, transforms the writers' regional identification; in different ways and in varying degrees, they all think of themselves as inheritors of distinct southern foodways traditions, but they, like Edward Lee, craft their own vision of what constitutes New Southern cooking though interaction with others according to three distinct narrative strategies:

1. **The creation of syncretic southern foodways in exile.** The late acclaimed poet Maya Angelou, author of *Hallelujah! The Welcome Table*, and Patty Pinner in her *Sweets: Soul Food Desserts & Memories*, both portray themselves as inheritors of a composite southern culinary tradition, soul food, which mixes and matches cooking styles and ethnic preferences. Both discuss the experience of cooking southern food while living in the North (Pinner) or out West (Angelou).
2. **The depiction of Miami as the culinary capital of the Cuban diaspora and, by extension, of South Florida as a new hub of the "Deep" South.** Food writers Mary Urrutia Randelman's *Memories of a Cuban Kitchen* and Viviana Carballo's *Havana Salsa: Stories and Recipes*, as well as playwright Eduardo Machado's *Tastes Like Cuba: An Exile's Hunger for Home*, all contend with Miami's status as the seat of power of the multigenerational Cuban American community and the mecca of a distinctively American, and southern, style of updating traditional Cuban cuisine.
3. **The portrayal of the borderlands as sites of contested difference within sameness.** Novelist Denise Chávez's *A Taco Testimony: Meditations on Family, Food and Culture* contrasts each of her parents' performances, or rejections, of their shared *mexicano* identity, even as Chávez herself adopts a more activist consciousness as a Chicana who celebrates her heritage and promotes the vibrant and productive material culture of the American Southwest.[1] However, the Chávez family taco

---

1. "Chicano" and "Chicana" are self-chosen designations often used by educated and politicized Mexican Americans who want to convey their solidarity with their working-class families and peers. It does not extend to other ethnicities.

fights constitute but one staging ground for this three-theater battle to reclaim Mexican cuisine for the Global South. The other two are Machado's discussion of intra-Latino tensions between Cubans and Mexicans in the era of Jim Crow and Maya Angelou's appropriation of Mexican cooking through her boasts about making a mean tamale. By incorporating Mexican dishes into their Cuban and soul food traditions or culinary repertoires, Machado and Angelou reinscribe this cuisine as a defining element of the evolving gastronomy of the New South.

Working against the trope of the American South as a place of stagnation and suffocating tradition that permeated literature and film in the second half of the twentieth century, these memoirs use food as the medium through which they reconstruct a New South as a symbol for their respective families' interpersonal relations. These memoirs' discussions of the cuisine of the New South take place against a background of the region's ongoing renaissance, which has had a profoundly humane dimension. The New South acknowledges and seeks to redress past wrongs while simultaneously embracing and reinvigorating traditions that many who had left had lost or felt forced to abandon.

In *Becoming Southern,* historian Christopher Morris points out that the South only attained its iconic status as the nation's borders kept shifting through the admission of more territories as states into the Union: "The South was more than an amalgam of distinct regions. It was a continually developing society. We understand well how the South varied from place to place. We are not so sure how it varied over time. Few studies present us with a picture of an evolving South" (Morris 1995, xv). This chapter is predicated precisely upon the notion of the New South as a region defined by the interactions between change and tradition, taking into account histories of migration, material culture, and people's affective reactions to the region. The food memoirs with recipes discussed here chronicle the hard work that goes into crafting the diverse communities that have given rise to the New South.

Their shared devotion to regionally inflected southern foodways—whether these are Mexican or Tex-Mex, Cuban American, or soul food—mark Angelou, Pinner, Urrutia Randelman, Carballo, Machado, and Chávez as members of the same New South in transition. Histories of migration, whether internal (across the United States) or external (from Cuba and Mexico), unite these memoirs around a mythical South that corresponds to, but also transcends, geographical boundaries. This timeless Dixie was constructed through the lens of gastronomic nostalgia; it was a site of local food production, where the connections between farm and table were clearly defined and families were involved in all aspects of feeding themselves, from growing food and raising pigs and poultry to canning, preserving, and preparing food. These writers interweave their personal genealogies with larger historical forces—from transatlantic slavery to Manifest Destiny and the Cold War fight against communism. The recipes included alongside the memoirs correspond to dishes that typify the cuisine of the family's country or state of origin and simultaneously serve as "authentic" representations of a regionally inflected yet diverse way of being "southern" in the New South. In downplaying the geopolitical differences that separate them, and instead emphasizing the similarity of experience within a shared territory common to all—the United States, where these dishes may be suitably recreated—these memoirs with recipes establish a textual borderland that temporarily encompasses reader and writer within the same imagined community, one that privileges the South as its culinary center.

Syncretic Southern Foodways in Exile

Historian James N. Gregory's *The Southern Diaspora* analyzes the impact of the departures of both African Americans and whites from the South after the Civil War, reading these overlapping Great Migrations out as an internal diaspora.[2] By reading the memoirs with recipes as texts bridging cultural gaps between southerners and those not from the South, I focus my discussion in this chapter on the dynamic, if not reciprocal, relationships they explicitly set up between an individual writer and his or her readers as joint participants in an intercultural exchange. One part of this exchange takes place when fellow southerners meet one another in a geographical location far removed from the South and bond over their shared appreciation of the region's famed foodways. Gregory credits Thomas Wolfe's novel *Look Homeward, Angel* with "establishing the trope of the southern writer in emotional exile" (2005, 184), but cautions that this literary depiction of homesickness has been used almost exclusively by white southern writers like Tennessee

---

2. If we consider the turbulent history of southern secession and the subsequent establishment of the Confederacy (1861–65) as a rival nation-state system to the United States of America, the existence of a distinct southern white exilic consciousness passed down the generations is not too dissimilar to the sense of displacement immigrants feel when leaving their country of origin. Thus, using the framework of immigration as a comparison to the departure from the South is an apt way to understand the lingering nostalgia felt by those who moved away.

Williams, rather than applied to, or claimed by, African Americans. In *Hallelujah! The Welcome Table*, Maya Angelou does just that when she includes an anecdote about finding common cause with a white, southern "emotional exile" in California. The white southerner's enjoyment of the simple traditional brunch Angelou prepares for him emphasizes that the South can be a place of interracial fellowship, even if only in the diaspora. This is an instance where a culinary performance—cooking—allows a young Angelou not only to find employment, but also to turn a little corner of California into a southern dining room for an evening, alleviating both her own and her employer's nostalgia for home.[3]

A friend arranged for Angelou to prepare brunch for Phil, a potential employer described as "a good ole white boy from the South . . . so homesick that he would break down and cry if you mentioned fried chicken" (Angelou 2004, 136). Angelou accepted the challenge and bought the provisions but refused to include grits, causing her friend and brunch host much consternation. When she announced the meal was ready and informed the inquisitive Phil that there were no grits, he was visibly disappointed, but then, Angelou revealed herself as a more authentically southern cook than the automatic inclusion of grits on the menu would have conveyed:

"I made spoon bread."

"Spoon bread. You said spoon bread? I haven't had spoon bread since I left Birmingham."

Seeing him so pleased delighted me. I added, "I make my own sausage, and we'll also have fried apples and homemade biscuits." His smile was so winning I could have hugged him. . . . He would put a forkful of food in his mouth and then he would seem to disappear. He slowly chewed his way back to his Alabama childhood. (Angelou 2004, 137)

This episode casts Phil's and Angelou's shared culinary citizenship in the Old South in an extremely positive light. It also, however, demonstrates

---

3. One of the chief tropes of southern white nostalgia in exile is the loss of the domestic space created by black servants. It is a constant source of reflection and a clear example of how poorly the all-American concept of the "nuclear family" fit particular situations—especially in its most conservative communities. Literary critic Doris Witt remarks upon the deep impact that his "actual memories of black domestics" (Witt 2004, 72) had upon Mississippi-born and -raised *New York Times* food critic and cookbook writer Craig Claiborne. In *Black Hunger,* she goes so far as to "hypothesize that the conscious figuration of a powerful black woman in the kitchen was necessary to enable the young, queer misfit 'Craig' to establish a coherent identity as 'Mr. Claiborne'" (Witt 2004, 72).

the power inequalities implicit in this encounter. On the one hand, Phil had relative wealth, power, and influence—he could hire Maya Angelou for a copywriting job at will if her cooking impressed him. On the other hand, only Angelou had the ability to make the very food for which he longed so dearly. Thus, she had the power to keep his food nostalgia at bay. This anecdote underscores the creative continuity that exists between cooking and writing as acts of performance and composition with a primary focus on audience. Angelou's agency is doubly affirmed, both in her performer role as a cook and in her authorial role in staging and ultimately setting the stakes of these significant interactions for a readership curious to understand the human dimensions of racial ideology in the United States. The vignette ends with the offer of employment, in exchange for Angelou's written recipe for spoon bread and the rest of the items served at brunch. Phil prophesied that if Angelou could write as well as she cooked, she had a bright future ahead of her. Given Maya Angelou's acclaimed career as a poet and writer, the reader of the memoir can be assured that the recipe included in the book will yield amazing results.

Hallelujah! The Welcome Table also contains another instance in which Angelou's talents in the kitchen helps her "pass" as a different kind of southerner than she is. She told a restaurant owner that Creole food "is all I know how to cook" (Angelou 2004, 77), despite never having been to Louisiana or tasted its food. On the merits of this boast, Angelou got the job, which provided sufficient income for her to pay her rent and still afford to have her infant son looked after. Although she bluffed her qualifications, she knew that she could learn the secrets of Creole cooking in short order from Papa Ford, the handyman in her mother's boarding house. While he hailed from Terre Haute, Indiana, Ford had traveled all around the country, working as a chef in the Merchant Marines and in Pullman cars. He revealed the secret to making Creole food: "Ain't nothing but onions, celery, green peppers, garlic, and tomatoes. Put that in everything and you got Creole food. I already told you how to cook rice" (Angelou 2004, 79). He then added the reminder to add red pepper to everything. Ford's description of Creole food at once essentialized it by conflating the cuisine with its ingredients, and it also rendered it universal by assuming that any cook with proper training and native skills could produce it. These instructions helped Angelou prosper at the job and please the regulars, whom she describes as "light-skinned, slick-haired Creoles from Louisiana, who spoke French patois only a little less complicated than the contents of my pots and equally spicy" (Angelou 2004, 79). This anecdote conveys the myriad ways in which the Old South was diverse, though not always legibly so to outsiders. As living reminders of the history of French colonialism in North America, Creoles (and Cajuns) represent yet another of the many diasporic populations that make up the South. Their histories of intermarriage and mixed race also constitute another challenge to the black-white color line that frames American race relations. Angelou's "Creole" cooking found favor with her customers, and that granted her the status of honorary Creole. In this instance of culinary impersonation, Maya Angelou got paid to cook differently than she ate, just so she had enough money to put food on the table for her young son.

Southern blacks who went North rather than West during the Great Migration often re-created communities similar to those they left behind by organizing their social activities through the local church in their new neighborhoods. Railroads and bus lines joining North and South made it feasible for families to visit one another, and for the children to be sent to spend time with their grandparents down South when school let out for the summer.[4] This gave rise to an internal revolving-door model of diaspora community foundation. An example of how Northern-born children were introduced to the joys of down-home cooking is Patty Pinner's *Sweets: Soul Food Desserts & Memories*, a memoir chock-full of recipes from her relatives' southern heritage. Although she was born and raised in Saginaw, Michigan, Pinner is the proud inheritor of her Mississippi grandmother's soul food recipes. She points out how a beloved dish can erase geographical divisions and bring people together, even in the chilly North.

Pinner's grandparents, Pop and My My, moved to Michigan from Mississippi to work in the burgeoning auto industry at the end of the 1940s. Rather than adapting to the culture of her new northern environs, My My set about re-creating the social ties and networks she had known and enjoyed in the South by preparing the same traditional meals the family was used to and joining the local church, which was a gathering place for other transplanted southerners. As Pinner recounts, "As it had been in the South, the church soon became an important part of My My's social life. And just as quickly, her food baskets—especially those holding her desserts—became as popular as they had been in Mississippi" (Pinner 2006, 2). Pinner's memoir is unique among the ones discussed throughout the rest of this book because it focuses exclusively on desserts and shares anecdotes primarily drawn from women's lives. By including the family recipes from relatives with roots in Mississippi and New Orleans, and describing

---

4. Emmet Till was the archetypal representative of the very real dangers this journey "home" to visit relatives in the South posed for northern black young men.

these with the more diasporic label of "soul food" rather than "southern cuisine," Pinner establishes her right to claim this southern cooking tradition in *Sweets*.

While most of Pinner's anecdotes and recipes come from her extended family, occasionally she tells stories about her grandmother's friends, among them Miss Drucilla, My My's best friend. This large woman made a yearly visit to Pinner's family by bus, a journey made more challenging by her considerable heft. Once she arrived, however, My My would greet her with her favorite dessert, lemon rum cake, and the two women would exchange stories "that made my grandmother giggle like a schoolgirl" (Pinner 2006, 48). Even as this ritual was repeated year after year, Drucilla and My My would argue good-heartedly about which of them could take credit for the lemon rum cake, since My My actually prepared it but Drucilla claimed the recipe as her own intellectual property. This playful exchange illustrates the degree to which cooking was serious business in determining how women got along with one another in social circumstances that centered around the kitchen.

A common culinary repertoire can also be used as a means of distinguishing oneself from others in the same community. Transplanted southern women showed off their culinary skills as a way of establishing their relative rank within a particular social circle, whether within the family or in the church community, as Psyche Williams-Forson explains in her book, *Building Houses Out of Chicken Legs*:

> Because most of the country churches were also devoid of any form of kitchen facilities, women would prepare the meals at home and, during a break in the service, would spread their meals on blankets and other coverings to serve. This allowed worshippers to enjoy not only the fellowship of the spirit but also the fellowship of the members whom they would see only during these occasions.
>
> Many black women seized this opportunity and used the church as a site to display their culinary skills, expand how they identified themselves, and contribute to African American cultural production. (Williams-Forson 2006, 136)

This passage, as well as the rest of Williams-Forson's book, demonstrates how time and again black women had to make a virtue out of necessity and relied on creativity to solve common problems like distance from home and lack of access to food preparation by pooling their resources, boosted by the spirit of a little friendly competition.

Since the church picnics were a regular social occasion, northern women who wished to properly uphold their reputation as good soul food cooks had to produce reliably good-tasting meals that could withstand the heat and waiting. Much in the same way that international diasporic communities stay in touch with one another through available mass-communication technologies, the telephone facilitated ongoing communications between family households separated by the southern diaspora, as was the case in Pinner's household:

> My My brought most of her recipes with her from the South; she carried many of them in her head. Occasionally, though, she would call home to one of her cousins or to one of her sisters (Sara, Bulah, Evelyn, Laura, or Eloise) who still lived down South, requesting something "new and different" for an upcoming church supper or a family gathering. My southern great-cousins and great-aunts were as dedicated to their culinary reputations as were their relatives transplanted to the North. . . . In no time, someone from "home" would call with the perfect recipe. (Finner 2006, 16)

This exchange of culinary knowledge was predicated upon an understanding that the relative who had migrated North would be representing the entire extended family, and their place of origin, through My My's cooking for fellow picnickers at the church; thus, it was important that the family agree upon what dish should be prepared because all of them were emotionally invested in the successful outcome of the food preparation. By watching this culinary collaboration between lifelong southerners and northern transplants, Pinner saw diasporic networks in action, and was lucky enough to taste the results.

While geographical borders, such as the one dividing North from South, can be overcome through the active cultivation of strong diasporic ties, over time the separation from the originary homeplace can lead community members to want to police the behavior of those who moved away in order to ensure their continued adherence to the "authentic" ways. Pinner gives one example of this surveillance in the anecdote that accompanies the recipe for "Aint Sug's Punkin Pie." While she lived down South, Aint Sug's gardens were renowned for their beauty. However, her response to finding a bug in her mother's garden made her the subject of intense scrutiny upon her return from Chicago:

> When she'd travel back home to visit, the folks down South would accuse her of having become uppity. They said that because Aint Sug had had a

little taste of city life, she thought she had become too good for the country. They'd claim she was "putting on airs" when they'd hear her blood-curling screams coming from her mother's garden—a mile away—each time an insect landed on her arm. The country folks couldn't understand how a woman born and raised in the country could be afraid of country critters. (Pinner 2006, 92)

This aspect of the revolving-door migration that characterized the mass movement out of the South helped police behavior both ways in patterns now seen between immigrants and their relatives in the countries of origin. Both sets of migrants bring back material goods from their northern abodes to make the lives of their relatives "back home" easier. They are expected to prove that their residence away from the South has not dampened their esteem for their birthplace or its tradition. Likewise, this social and moral surveillance of immigrants by their families and migrants by their country relatives is premised upon the notion that the "traditional" customs will soon be judged to be backwards by the returnees and in need of change or adaptation to the mores of the more "advanced" times. New migrants North or West also faced scrutiny by their more established friends and relatives, holding them responsible for assimilating to city ways quickly and coping with entirely new circumstances of which they were previously unaware. As tense as these exchanges were, or could be, they nonetheless demonstrate the effort involved in keeping a diaspora community alive and engaged with "home."

A similar dynamic of policing authenticity and proper behavior through eating and cooking is at play in Miami, the home of the largest Cuban community in the United States. Mary Urrutia Randelman's family immigrated to the United States before Castro came to power; Machado and Carballo left after the Cuban Revolution. He was a child whose exit was negotiated through the Catholic Church's relief organization, Operation Pedro Pan,[5] whereas Viviana Carballo left as an adult after successfully applying for an exit visa. Once they each arrived in the United States, Urrutia Randelman, Viviana Carballo, and Eduardo Machado had to contend, in some way or another, with the Miami community as the arbiters of Cuban American respectability and culinary authenticity. I suggest that their memoirs depict Miami as a social and cultural force to be reckoned with, which posits South Florida at the heart of a newly constituted and transnational "Deep" South.

---

5. See Triay 1999. For a collection of personal accounts by Pedro Pan children, see Conde 2000.

Miami as the Culinary Capital of the Cuban Diaspora and the "Deep" South

Mary Urrutia Randelman speaks about Miami exile life with absolute ease, as someone whose culinary citizenship in the Miami food scene is unproblematic and secure despite her departure from the South, first to New York City in 1958, and eventually to Los Angeles, where she and her American-born, Cuban-raised white husband settled down.[6] Urrutia Randelman's *Memories of a Cuban Kitchen* is organized according to the kinds of foods it discusses instead of using a schema that follows the author's life in Cuba. Like *Havana Salsa*, Urrutia Randelman's book unabashedly celebrates her childhood on the island and the meals she enjoyed as a member of the privileged upper class. However, whereas Carballo reveals her anger at the deprivation she suffered during the early years of the Cuban Revolution and her decision to leave, Urrutia Randelman skips right over anything that might seem the slightest bit political, despite being the daughter of a Cuban politician. She hides behind the veil of childhood to convey her complete surprise that her family boarded a ship one sunny day in Cuba and later docked in Miami. Like Carballo, Urrutia Randelman paints a portrait of Old Cuba as a multicultural society, and its cuisine as "Creole or *comidas criollas*," defining it as

> an amalgam of tropical and European elements. It is based on the white sweet potatoes, squash, corn and yucca that had been cultivated by early Taino and Siboney Indian inhabitants and later were adopted by the African slaves; on Spanish saffron, rice, beans and *sofritos* (simmered sauces) combining garlic, onion, pepper and tomato; on Indian and Chinese culinary contributions; and, finally on the fish, meats, vegetables, and herbs native to our island. (Urrutia Randelman and Schwartz 1992, 1–2)

This definition of Cuban food strangely effaces the agrarian labor that produces all of the listed foodstuffs, even those "native to our island," which must nonetheless be cultivated in order to be available to all. What Urrutia Randelman does emphasize, however, is its fusion of distinct culinary traditions, thereby implicitly acknowledging the island's history of imperialism,

---

6. I will follow Latino precedent here and refer to Mary Urrutia Randelman by both of her surnames, since to use only her husband's last name would not fully capture her subject position as a married Cuban American woman. Her full name appears on the cover of her book, in contrast to Vivana Carballo, who has reverted to using her maiden name after two divorces. I respect her choice in my references to her.

displacement of Native cultures, transatlantic slavery, indentured servitude, and immigration.

One of the distinguishing factors between the Old Cuban way of cooking and its Miami interpretation is the emphasis on convenience foods readily available to serve busy families. Urrutia Randelman celebrates the fissures, the places where the illusion of Miami as the same or equivalent to Havana shatter, such as in the Cuban bakeries, which prepare both old standbys like *"croquetas, cangrejitos, pastelitos, empanadas* and many variations of *bocaditos"* along with uncanny adaptations of dishes that fit within a modern lifestyle, like premade *"bocadito* fillings (*pastas de bocadito*) so you can prepare your own 'tiny mouthful' at home" (Urrutia Randelman and Schwartz 1992, 21). The chapter discussing *"Lechón Asado"* juxtaposes Cuban and Cuban American ways to prepare the traditional roast pork, the typical Christmas meal:

> In Cuba, the traditional Christmas pigs were roasted over open fires or prepared by local restaurants for families to take home. In Miami, families can buy their roasts ready-cooked, or they can take oven-ready pigs, seasoned at home, to bakeries that prepare the roasts in their large ovens. You can roast this little pig at home, since it only weighs ten to fifteen pounds, but you must order it specially [sic] from the butcher and take some care in its preparation. (Urrutia Randelman and Schwartz 1992, 131)

Urrutia Randelman's discussion of both approaches to preparing Christmas pork presents them as equivalent, without privileging one as inherently more authentic than the other. The central place of pork in this culinary tradition constitutes common ground between it and traditional southern and southwestern foodways. This is one aspect that would make the South seem less foreign for immigrants arriving from the Caribbean, and therefore make these same new arrivals somewhat more legible to their neighbors. Since she left the island as a child with her parents before Fidel Castro came to power, and then later married an American man, Urrutia Randelman's view of the Cuban exiles versus Cuban American diasporic community divide is predicated on celebrating continuity rather than pausing to reflect on rupture. Ironically, at the time of the memoir's publication, Urrutia Randelman was in exile from this "Deep South" capital, having relocated to Los Angeles, where there is a small but thriving Cuban American community. As with Maya Angelou and Patti Pinner, the book's publication allowed Mary to conjure up her memories of both Cuba and Cuban Miami from the site of her "emotional" exile.

In contrast, Carballo's identification with the island of her birth in this memoir is unapologetically atemporal; *Havana Salsa* only discusses the meals Carballo enjoyed when she lived in her beloved city, even though her personal experience at this time was based more on eating what her parents, grandparents, or hired cooks prepared at home or the meals served in the restaurants the family patronized, than from any hands-on experience actually preparing the meals herself. Like Madhur Jaffrey and Cheryl Lu-Lien Tan, Viviana was neither interested in mastering nor required to learn the art of Cuban home cooking as a young girl. Only as her wedding date neared did her mother finally give the young woman a crash course in home economics, imparting upon her just enough culinary know-how to start out married life. Carballo left Cuba soon after the Bay of Pigs invasion. The vehemence with which she distances herself from the island Cubans marks her as a member of the Cuban exile community in the United States, even if she never explicitly counts herself among their number within the memoir.

As a political exile, Viviana Carballo chose to leave her birthplace to escape the repressive policies that followed the Cuban Revolution; thus, she views cooking the food she knew and loved from her childhood as a way to mitigate her homesickness and stake a claim to the island's heritage by preserving the cherished culinary traditions. Not coincidentally, this distance and longing for home helped her become a culinary expert, mastering the region's distinctive tastes: Carballo's occupation as a food columnist for the *Orlando Sentinel* and *Miami Herald* made her something of a liaison between the bilingual Cuban exile community in South Florida and their U.S.-born children and grandchildren. The recipes she shares with her readers reflect those long-gone days more than they correspond to the contemporary cuisine of the South (Miami) at the time when *Havana Salsa* was published. Since Carballo had no children of her own, *Havana Salsa* serves to pass on her culinary legacy to the younger generation of Cuban Americans, as well as among the millions of non-Cuban foodies who enjoy eating *medianoche* sandwiches or *ropa vieja* stew in any of the countless Cuban restaurants that have sprung up in Florida and elsewhere throughout the United States. Mexican pozole soup, German pancakes, and white gazpacho were served in her household, alongside more traditional offerings like oxtail stew, fried green plantains (*tostones*), and coconut flan (custard). By sharing her recollections about the central role that food played in southern or Cuban cuisine when she lived there, Carballo educates the next generation of cooks, who will presumably then add their own spin on "classic" dishes like *ajiaco* or vegetable stew (Carballo 2006, 221). In updating these old standbys, home cooks as much as professional chefs can perform their own culinary citizenship and stake their claims to the New South.

Carballo sees Miami through the lens of her political exile; it seems like the least unlike-home place in the United States to live. Carballo explicitly addresses herself in the introduction to an audience of non-Latinos and second-generation Cuban Americans, like her "U.S.-born nephews and nieces [who] ask me to tell them stories of the Cuba I lived in" (Carballo 2006, xiv). They have eaten the Cuban food their aunt prepares, heard about the Caribbean island's wonders, and learned about its tumultuous political history without visiting it themselves. Thus, for Carballo, kinship functions as a framework through which to pass on her culinary heritage, but she takes no chances and embraces the role and responsibility of being a cultural translator to the American reading public who may want to acquire such culinary citizenship as well. This effort to connect with her younger, non-Cuban audiences who value diversity and multiculturalism is a conscious decision meant to pass on her memories of the homeland to a younger generation.

Despite these overt instances where Carballo reaches out to non-Cuban readers, she also downplays her own experience of life in the United States; *Havana Salsa* is largely silent about her life in Florida after her arrival in 1961. The American foodscape against which *Havana Salsa* presents Cuban food is not one where down-home southern staples like fried chicken, okra, collard greens, or sweet tea were prevalent; instead, she contrasts the warm and flavorful homemade meals of her childhood with the government-issued, unappealing mass-produced foods she received as a political refugee: "many pounds of Spam, a military-size can of powdered eggs, and an enormous log of processed cheese" (Carballo 2006, 249). This efficient bounty nourished the exile, but did little to win over her taste buds or stomach to the American way of life. Exile, whether emotional or political, is a common thread linking the three versions of the New South under discussion here. For Carballo, as it was for Phil, the white southerner for whom Angelou cooked, recollections of a long-lost home are wrapped up in nostalgia for the foodways associated with it and the servants who prepared those beloved dishes. Part of the appeal of the South is its cultural reluctance to simply forget, or to forget simply. It does not share the wider American impulse to forge ahead or look forward.[7]

---

7. It is an ironic dimension that the "lost cause" of the South can appeal to outsiders like Carballo who do not share its political agenda, but value tradition for its own sake. Her anger at Fidel Castro permeates every page of this memoir with recipes; by preserving the recipes of the cuisine she associates with the golden age of Cuba before

Whereas Carballo left Cuba after she had learned to cook and gotten married, Machado and Urrutia Randelman were children at the time of their departure.[8] Machado's and Urrutia Randelman's depiction of their younger selves in *Tastes Like Cuba* and *Memories of a Cuban Kitchen* focus on their role as eating subjects, rather than as cooks, thereby broadening their appeal to readers who themselves are not adept in the kitchen. Thus, the claims of kitchen expertise or gastronomic authority implicit within these memoirs come from their later mastery of traditional Cuban recipes, kitchen skills they developed while living in the United States. These two memoirs affirm that Cuban cuisine is part and parcel of American life, but they do so from different perspectives. Whereas Carballo wants to isolate her memories of Cuba from her life in exile, Urrutia Randelman takes a syncretic view of border crossing, regarding her childhood on the island and her exile in Miami as two sides of the same coin. Machado, in contrast, has a broader perspective on Latino life in the United States, having spent his youth among Mexican Americans and Chicanos in Los Angeles and his adult life surrounded by Dominicans and Puerto Ricans in New York, with occasional visits to the Miami-based Cuban community.

Whereas Urrutia Randelman's *Memories of a Cuban Kitchen* promotes Miami as the American headquarters or home base for the Cuban diaspora in the United States, and Carballo's *Havana Salsa* is an expanded version of the anecdotes she told her American-born nieces and nephews, Machado's *Tastes Like Cuba* recounts three parallel transformations he undergoes in the United States: the first is from Cuban child to Cuban American adult; the second is from aspiring actor to successful playwright; and the third is from identifying as a straight man married to an older woman to coming out as gay and establishing a household with his younger partner, Michael Domitrovich.[9] *Tastes Like Cuba* is a hybrid text: at times it reads like a travelogue;

---

the Revolution, Carballo is still fighting her own "lost cause" against the Communist takeover of her island.

8. Urrutia Randelman's family left the island before the Cuban Revolution. Machado and his younger brother left after the Revolution, once Castro had taken over all private industries. Machado and his brother soon made the journey to the United States ahead of their parents, but in the company of many other refugee children who were evacuated from the island as part of Operation Pedro Pan. This program was cosponsored by the United States government and the Catholic Church to facilitate the departure of Cuban children from the island. Upon arrival in the United States, the children resided in church-led orphanages until they could be reunited with relatives.

9. Domitrovich shares some of the writing credit on the memoir. In the author bio listed on the back cover, Machado's partner, Michael, mentions having grown up in a family of restaurateurs, thereby implying that the nature of his contribution to this project was primarily focused on recipe testing.

in other instances it is a coming out story. Early chapters detail the Machado family's rags-to-riches story in Cuba, and yet the middle sections describe the hardship of apartment living in an ethnic enclave in Los Angeles. Machado's writing talent is in ample evidence: he has a great ear for dialogue and frames each chapter as a scene in a larger dramatic narrative that has elements of suspense, intrigue, tragedy, and joy, all punctuated by scrumptious recipes for the Dominican, Mexican, and Haitian dishes his family learned to prepare after settling down Stateside, as well as the occasional southern specialty (pecan pie) and example of early California cuisine ("hippie salad"). Mostly, however, the featured recipes are for traditional and beloved Cuban dishes like black beans, *bacalao* (salt cod), and *arroz con pollo* (rice with chicken), to name a few, as well as the requisite cocktails (mojitos and Cuba libre) and the dessert that gave the title to his most famous dramatic trilogy: "floating islands."

Machado occupies multiple border identities at once without ever feeling like he fully belongs anywhere: he is an artist who makes his living as an academic (he is a professor at Columbia); he writes plays that are produced in both Spanish and English but are never fully embraced by either the exile generation or younger, Cuban American audiences; he grew up in Los Angeles, lives in New York, and is not embraced by the Cuban exile establishment in Miami. He openly discusses his subject position as an itinerant dweller in the major metropolitan Latino centers of the United States—Miami, New York, and Los Angeles—but is welcomed back to the island of his birth by virtue of the artistic acclaim and recognition he has earned in the United States. *Tastes Like Cuba* explains the significance of both food and cuisine to Machado's literary portrayal of Cuban society on stage. Unlike Carballo, who feels disconnected from island Cubans and does not discuss her life in the United States in the memoir, or Urrutia Randelman, who plays a role as a spokesperson for the Miami Cuban community even from the distance of her Los Angeles home, Machado's success as a playwright in New York made it possible for him first to return to Cuba and share his artistic works with his countrymen and, eventually, to obtain a contract to publish his food memoir in the United States. The scope of Machado's *Tastes Like Cuba* is larger than that of *Havana Salsa,* and features a more sustained interaction with Cuban cuisine, past and present. Though Eduardo Machado lacks the benefit of Carballo's formal training in the culinary arts, he has nonetheless made food a central theme of his creative depictions of life in Cuba and the struggles of Cuban Americans during his long career as a playwright. This acknowledged gap in his background suggests that instead of actual family recipes passed down to him through the generations, those included in *Tastes Like Cuba* are almost entirely apocryphal versions, contemporary reinterpretations of beloved family dishes from his youth or delicious entrées sampled during his visits to Cuban *paladares*, or private home-based restaurants Castro allowed to set up business during the early years of the special period.[10] The literal translation of the Spanish word *paladar* means "palate." Machado's repeated visits to Cuba mark the playwright as a cultural translator who shows both island- and Miami-based Cuban communities glimpses of how the other half lives and eats.

Emboldened by the success of his artistic endeavors, as well as by a brand-new love, Machado decided to give Miami another try and agreed to have his play *Once Removed* staged in Coconut Grove at the request of Lucie Arnaz, the daughter of Hollywood royalty Desi Arnaz and Lucille Ball. Machado and Arnaz collaborated on a rewrite of the play, and the process made him feel less apprehensive about the play's reception: "Heading down to Miami, arm in figurative arm with Lucie, I felt like none of the Cubans would be able to stop us—not the exiles, not the critics, not even my family" (Machado and Domitrovich 2007, 313). This acceptance from a prominent member of the Miami Cuban American community made it easier for Machado to imagine separating his mixed feelings about parts of his family who lived in Miami from his attitude toward the city that had most kept Cuban culture alive in the United States. Given that everything else in this memoir relates to food, this epiphany takes place while he and his partner, Michael, are eating:

> The flavors were still too strong, too salty, too garlicky. Both Michael and I usually ended up with big tummy aches after scarfing down the fried plantain discs and fried beef. Garlic burps, swollen tongues, and headaches. I

---

10. While he is perhaps best known as the author of the *Floating Island* plays, in which food figures prominently as part of the Cuban family's daily life, Machado's most explicit dramaturgical exploration of the central role food plays in the Cuban communities of both the island and the diaspora may be found in the play *The Cook*. It is based on a woman Machado met when he visited her *paladar*, or privately owned restaurant run out of her house, during a return trip to Cuba as a featured artist in residence. It features a character who prepares meals onstage before a live audience as she recites her lines and moves about the set. When he discusses this woman and the process of writing the play within the pages of *Tastes Like Cuba*, the episode becomes a meditation upon the sacrifice of the Cuban citizens who either endured or threw in their lot behind the Revolution, as well as the small but increasing concessions they have begun to enjoy since the declaration of the special period, such as the right to engage in commerce by selling home-grown produce at local farmers' markets or running *paladares* out of their homes.

knew I was back in South Florida. But something had changed. I no longer cared that Miami didn't quite live up to the Cuba of my mind. How could it? It was Miami. Not Cuba. It was on that trip that I learned to take the goodness where I could find it. We ate *Vaca Frita* and *tostones* with reckless abandon. The swollen tongues and aching bellies were part of the experience.

And so Miami began to feel more and more like home. (Machado and Domitrovich 2007, 314)

While the show's premiere went well, the trip itself was the biggest success because Machado made peace with his Miami relatives and used his art to claim a space within the city that was uniquely his, rather than indebted to their influence. Likewise, having spent enough time in twenty-first-century Cuba, Machado finally let go of his assumption that Miami should somehow measure up to Havana and accepted it for what it is: a southern outpost of the Cuban diaspora. This meal shared with his Russian American lover conveys the couple's performance of a joint Cuban culinary citizenship; it also foreshadows the supporting role Michael would play as Machado's coauthor of *Tastes Like Cuba*.

The Borderlands as Sites of Contested Difference within Sameness

Novelist Denise Chávez's memoir, *A Taco Testimony,* suggests that the opposite of the multicultural and diverse New South could be a Southwest obsessed with the vanity of small differences where no one can claim culinary membership because everyone's idea of what is authentic is at odds. Chávez's fixation with her family history is almost disenabling because she cannot ultimately resolve her dilemma: what kind of Southwestern woman is she? We already know she considers herself as a "Mexican," without reference to either whiteness or indigeneity, and yet she chooses to continue living in her father's home state rather than her mother's. Her home's proximity to the United States–Mexico border, together with the example her mother set of helping those less fortunate, means that Chávez finds herself and her citizenship challenged throughout her life:

> I know borders, real and imagined. I know what it is to have the rabia/ anger, the unmitigated rage well up and then subside, wondering how I will enunciate my rights yet another time. Will I be waved away, dismissed

or interrogated? "American citizen," I hear myself say in a faraway voice. "I am an American citizen." (Chávez 2006, 172)

To make matters more confusing, she eventually moves into her childhood home as an adult after the death of her mother. This level of willful mimesis or duplication of her past with some room for difference is evident in the memoir's design as well. *A Taco Testimony* is divided into sections that accord with the various parts of a formal meal, from a bracing "Aperitivo/ Aperitif" (Chávez 2006, 13), all the way through to "Sobritas/Leftovers" (Chávez 2006, 188). There are more poems interspersed throughout the chapters than there are actual recipes. Yet the final section is framed as if it were an actual taco-making workshop, discussing everything from Mexican myths of origin about corn to how to select good taco meat and providing a step-by-step guide on how to make corn tortillas. Because of its placement at the very end of the book and the unusual nature of the intertexts included within the memoir, it is unlikely that any but the most undaunted reader will stick around to finally learn how to make the titular delicacy.

Chávez has spent the majority of her life in the same place where she grew up: New Mexico. However, what makes her memoir suited for discussion in the context of imaginary constructs of a culinary New South is the fact that she recalls feeling constantly torn between her divorced parents' affective connections to different parts of the Southwest: her mother was a proud daughter of West Texas, while her father was devoted to his natal New Mexico. Each geographical location also conveys an attendant performance of race or ethnicity, like this exchange between father and daughter:

> I once asked my Father what his ethnicity was. He told me without hesitation that he was a "Spanish white man." My Mother, along with the rest of us, alas, was Mexican. And, even worse than being a Mexican, my Mother was a Texan. I don't think my Father ever forgave her for her overweening sense of pride in being from over there, that other place, Texas. (Chávez 2006, 78)

Chávez's father's self-definition also illustrates intra-Latino prejudice, which is its own form of the politics of respectability. Implied within this paragraph is the suggestion that the label "Mexican" is code for "indigenous," as opposed to "Spanish," like her father, and therefore, not white. Thus, although it is in a roundabout way, the color line once again makes its presence known within the family unit. Their love of rolled tacos was something they could at least agree on. "Respectability" and "dignity" are code words for "whiteness," which different Latino groups claim for themselves while denying to others, on whom they look down for their indigenous or African ancestry. In this instance, Chávez's father chose to embrace whiteness through the claim to a "Spanish" rather than Mexican heritage.

Since both of her parents are long dead and neither overcame his or her prejudices, Chávez turns to one of her mother's recipes, the one for "Delfina's Spanish—Really Mexican—Rice" (Chávez 2006, 75) to strike out against yet another manifestation of racism that oppressed her as a child. In the prefatory notes to the recipe, Chávez introduces the notion of "food racism":

> Mexicanos can never make Spanish rice; they can only make Mexican rice. Mexicans can make arroz al estilo Español but really what they make best is their own rice. Many people won't admit to being Mexican. They consider themselves Spanish. What can I say? This has led to a confusion of rice among other things. As for me, I consider myself a Mexicana/Americana/Chicana. So what kind of rice do I make? Let's not get lost in semantics of nationalism. And yet, let us celebrate who we really are. (Chávez 2006, 77–78)

This heated diatribe against the term "Spanish rice" to describe the type of rice dish made with tomatoes, onions, and chicken broth is a larger complaint against the whitewashing of Mexican identity in the Southwest. Chávez suggests that this prejudice is manifested down to the culinary level, and yet this is precisely the moment where her own prejudices against the type of "hippie health food" Eduardo Machado ate during his California marriage interrupt the internal logic of her semiotic critique against the use of "Spanish" as a shorthand for "whiteness."

After listing the ingredients for the dish and explaining the steps involved in the preparation, Chávez addresses herself directly to the reader in a challenging and combative tone. Chávez may find her father's self-description as a "Spanish white man" offensive, since it implies he sees himself as being a descendant of the Spanish colonizers rather than the colonized indigenous Mexicans, but the idea that anyone would choose to eat brown rice over her beloved white rice seems downright appalling to her, despite brown being the color associated with "mestizos," or people of mixed Spanish and indigenous heritage: "If you use brown rice, we know what kind of person you are, and it will take longer, about 45 minutes" (Chávez 2006, 78). There is no explanation of who the disapproving "we" with whom Chávez aligns herself are; this collective pronoun could include the reader if he or she does not plan on preparing this recipe with brown rice. The rice's "brownness" is objectionable in this context presumably because it is a symbol of wealth and privilege: only people who can afford to be concerned about improving their health would have the money and extra time to eat such an aesthetically inferior grain. The cook's own brownness, however, is valuable inasmuch as it demonstrates his or her claim to a Mexican identity rather than privileging white, European lineage. This is yet another instance in which the writer works out of a Latino politics of respectability that nonetheless hides some culinary intolerance.

A slightly different type of intra-Latino prejudice that overlaps with Jim Crow politics in the South is at work in Machado's *Tastes Like Cuba*. Eduardo Machado recalls a family road trip in the mid-1960s as an example of both how much his family's Cuban-ness troubled the black-white color line and how southern eateries were often the battlegrounds for this racial policing in the Old South. As they drove through Texas, the Machados felt insulted when the Mexican taco-stand operators confused them with their countrymen. Somehow, although the family was willing to eat the burritos and tacos they purchased, they did not welcome the idea that such consumption, in addition to their shared Spanish language, bestowed upon them a Mexican culinary citizenship, if only temporarily.

> We drove til nine o'clock, then stopped at a roadside motel. We ate burritos and tacos from a shack next door. The stand was owned by Mexicans who spoke Spanish to us and gave us a free Coca-Cola.
>
> The motel was not anywhere nearly as nice as a Holiday Inn. There was no pool. My father triple-locked the door, even placing a chair against it.
>
> The next morning he said, "Let's just get the hell out of Texas."
>
> "Really?" my mother said in a very sarcastic tone.
>
> "You were right. Even the Mexicans think we are Mexicans."
>
> "Wetbacks!" Mother exclaimed. She was angry. (Machado and Domitrovich 2006, 165)

While the Machados' putative whiteness afforded them a limited measure of privilege in some states, in others, like Louisiana, the Machados were directed to a motel for "colored" only, where the kids played in the pool with the children of the other guests, all of whom were black. When they went to a restaurant, the family was served dinner, but encouraged to take their dessert "to go," since the father's "arms and face were tanned and a deep brown. With his thick snarl of unwashed kinky hair, he almost looked like a mulatto" (Machado and Domitrovich 2006, 166). It was only after this experience that the elder Machados realized that their Cuban-ness did not signify in the South or Southwest—that their accents marked them as "Mexican" in the latter, and the father's skin color and hair texture were read as "black" in the former. For the rest of the journey, the family packed their own food so as to avoid undergoing the racial scrutiny at other eating establishments. Only in Miami did they feel properly recognized as "Cubans." Machado's retelling of this key event of his childhood still retains some trace of his incredulity about how American prejudice could be so color-blind as to fail to differentiate between Mexicans, Cubans, and African Americans, considering all of them equally "not-white."

As much as Urrutia Randelman, Carballo, and Machado add Cuban cuisines and exilic culture to the mixture of traditions that have reenergized southern foodways in the late twentieth century, Maya Angelou adds Mexican cuisine to the equation by proclaiming her own penchant for cooking it. This comes in the context of helping a friend prepare her boyfriend's favorite dish, tamales, in the hope that he would propose to her. According to Angelou, the suitor had some pretty high standards for his favorite food: "he loved Mexican food and he thought only some California Mexicans and a few Texas Mexicans could prepare tamales properly" (Angelou 2004, 127). Her friend, M. J., asked the poet to come supervise her culinary efforts, to ensure that the evening went off without a hitch because "she knew I cooked Mexican food often" (Angelou 2004, 128). Unlike the vignette about Creole food, in this instance Angelou portrays herself as a confident and competent cook whose renown in the kitchen is widespread. Maya Angelou feels absolutely no compunction or sense of either racial masquerading or appropriation in sharing her recipe for tamales in *Hallelujah! The Welcome Table*. Although she does not go so far as to praise her own skills directly, since her role in this occasion is supervisory rather than participatory, the end result is that the so-called tamale "expert" boyfriend proposes to M. J. upon trying her tamales. Thus, the implication is that under Angelou's tutelage, the food her friend produced was at least as good as that of "California Mexicans" or "Texas Mexicans." The recipe for "*Tamales de Maíz con Pollo* or Green Cornhusk Tamales with Chicken filling" (Angelou 2004, 131) is all Angelou's, however.

As represented and reimagined by these memoirs with recipes, *Hallelujah! The Welcome Table, Sweets, Memories of a Cuban Kitchen, Havana Salsa, Tastes Like Cuba,* and *A Taco Testimony*, the New South is a region full of contradictions: it simultaneously invites culinary innovation while preserving its multiple and storied cooking traditions; it has a long history of warm hospitality that has not always been extended to those whose skin was not white; and it is geographically defined, yet endures as an idea with deep emotional significance for both people who live there and those who have left. Thus, as a microcosm of American society at large, the New South has become a space where immigrants can gain a foothold and make a home while enjoying, and reshaping, the nation's tastiest regional foodways.

Chapter 4

Expats in Love
Recipes for Belonging Abroad

Read together, Kim Sunée's *Trail of Crumbs,* Colette Rossant's *The World in My Kitchen,* Linda Furiya's *How to Cook a Dragon,* and Jen Lin-Liu's two volumes *Serve the People* and *On The Noodle Road* suggest that a person's alimentary and sexual identities are best understood as intertwined manifestations of the embodied, desiring self within the economy of the household, especially when living abroad as expatriates. Thus, in recalling bygone feasts and their interactions with a (now-lost) beloved, these memoirists relive the pleasures afforded them by each, while also outlining the cost or price of achieving self-control over their physical and emotional appetites. These texts' overt focus on food allows these women to reclaim their own part of expatriate life—its tastes, smells, and culinary secrets—and to turn their newfound expertise in foreign or local cuisine into the basis for their own writing careers. By recalling life abroad through the lens of their respective romances and including recipes for dishes they ate, learned to prepare, or served at home during these times, these immigrant memoirs celebrate the appetites and speak joyfully of the pleasures to be had at the table and in bed. Their books, each in its own way, address the difficulty of living abroad as women whose outward appearance does not conform to the blond-haired, blue-eyed stereotype that so many cultures share when they imagine Americans. This awareness of the inadequacy of conventional labels and attitudes add a dimension of sensitivity and insight into their writing about foreign/local cuisines. Sunée, Rossant, Furiya, and Lin-Liu agree that finding one's place as an expatriate abroad should not come at the expense of other people's ability to tell their own stories; they share their personal anecdotes and recipes with their audiences without implying that the culinary traditions out of which they grow are anyone's for the taking.

In order to chronicle how the writers simultaneously affirm and perform their American-ness, the memoirs emplot their experience abroad according to two overlapping narrative arcs: a gastronomic odyssey and a feminist romance. The first is a script of gastronomic tourism, where the writers assume the role of what philosopher Lisa Heldke calls "food adventurers" by describing their overseas surroundings for their American readers eager to learn more about "foreign" foodways. Each woman's appetite gives her entry into an American subgroup of the rising class of global food enthusiasts: those who become devotees of a specific country's cuisine because of a perceived lack of an identifiable national cuisine of their own. *Trail of Crumbs, The World in My Kitchen, How to Cook a Dragon, Serve the People,* and *On The Noodle Road* speak directly to the anxiety American women feel about finding love and professional fulfillment even as their authors' status as naturalized or ethnic citizens brings ancillary hot-button social issues, like interracial romance, divorce, and abortion, to the forefront of their discussions of food and relationships experienced abroad. In the second narrative emplotment, the memoirists portray themselves as feminist romance heroines attempting to preserve their independence while living abroad under the auspices of their employed romantic partner. In their writing, Sunée, Rossant, Furiya, and Lin-Liu adopt what I call a collective "coupled-self" narrative persona through the use of the first-person plural pronoun "we" that filters all of the commentary on food and the experience of expatriation through the lens of a relational, affective identity as one half of a couple. Their discussions of the foods they ate and the places they traveled and lived in allow these four narrators to come to terms with their multiple and overlapping identities as ethnic American women who know whom and what they love and are not afraid to go after it.

Food Adventurers

In her book *Exotic Appetites: Ruminations of a Food Adventurer*, Lisa Heldke defines food adventurers, a group among whose members she counts herself, as often Euroamerican, Christian-raised persons for whom immigration is a (relatively) distant event—something undertaken by great grandparents, perhaps. We often find the foods that we ate growing up or that we eat on a daily basis to be boring; we long to spice up our diets (literally) with the flavors of exotic cuisines." (Heldke 2005, xxi)

Perhaps because they feel stuck in place, or just somewhat disconnected from their family's heritage, food adventurers find themselves drawn to other people's written accounts of arriving upon America's shores, ready to make a new future, as long as these tales contain ample references to the food they ate while making this transition. While Heldke specifies that not all food adventurers are white, she explicitly warns against trying to understand the experience of food adventurers of color through the frame of white privilege. Thus, it might be tempting to posit that the process of becoming a "food adventurer," when immigrants and/or their descendants actively seek out other tastes and spice combinations than those with which they are familiar, functions as a marker or benchmark of acculturation to mainstream American society and its bland or unremarkable cuisine. Yet this very formulation is tenuous at best because, as Heldke cautions, even "food adventurers" may act as agents of "cultural forms of food colonialism" (Heldke 2005, xx), because partaking of the cuisine of other groups, whether in restaurants or by following recipes from a cookbook or memoir with recipes, constitutes a form of appropriation.

By refining their own cooking skills, Sunée, Rossant, Furiya, and Lin-Liu link the legitimacy of their respective claims to both a place within the American imagined community as well as to their status as homemakers who turn their time in the kitchen into full-fledged writing careers. Rossant, Sunée, Furiya, and Lin-Liu make the day-to-day experiences of keeping house abroad the overt subject of their respective memoirs with recipes. However, the resultant texts are not simply panegyrics to the newfound glories of domestic bliss. They do not seek to establish a connection with their readers on the basis of an assumed similarity of lifestyle, but instead posit themselves as latter-day feminist expatriates trying to juggle culture shock, love, and new languages while eating some tasty food. Preparing and enjoying local dishes while living abroad allows the writers to explore the limits of their sense of personal and social belonging, even as they strive to sustain both love and friendship in these memoirs. Despite, or perhaps because of, their common emphasis on the household as the organizing principle that grounds these women's experience abroad in the cyclical time of food preparation and the changing of the seasons, these memoirs also track the writers' emotional and professional growth and independence, as measured by their increasingly sophisticated palates.

These memoirs triangulate each woman's racial and ethnic backgrounds (Asian American or Sephardic Jewish/French) with their American citizenship and their status as "expats" in order to establish a connection with their readers. These writers deploy recipes for "Sautéed Fiddlehead Ferns with Pomegranate" (*World in My Kitchen*), "Tea Infused Eggs" (*Serve the People*), "Dill and Fava Bean Pilaf" (*On the Noodle Road*), "Almond-Saffron Cake" (*Trail of Crumbs*), and "Lion Cub's Head Meatballs with Vegetables and Pasta" (*How to Cook a Dragon*), among others, as gateways to adventurous eating and vicarious travel for their readers, who can follow the steps and arrive at a gustatory destination very much like that undertaken by the writers themselves. In their eagerness to prepare and eat foods from many places, these writers most effectively perform their American-ness both for their immediate audiences made up of friends and acquaintances, as well as for their readers.

Instead of celebrating mobility itself, Rossant's, Sunée's, Furiya's, and Lin-Liu's narratives chronicle the experience of dwelling abroad by describing food within the context of the domestic households they established in Tanzania, Provence, and Beijing, respectively. The recipes included in each of these volumes bridge the distance between the readers' local homespace and their access to flavors from around the world, especially since the writers do not limit themselves to including recipes only from the national cuisine of the place where they reside as expatriates but also include others gathered while on their travels elsewhere. The protagonists of these food memoirs describe the time they spent living in foreign countries where they have developed affective connections through professional connections, personal friendships, love affairs, and heartbreak as especially memorable, in light of how the experience helped them hone their writing skills and find their own voice within their relationships and as ethnic Americans. The texts likewise converge in depicting the ethnic American expatriate as the central figure who is asked to prove or perform her nationality for local audiences who insist upon reading the memoirists' bodies—their spoken accents, facial features, hair—as texts that somehow contradict the women's claims to American citizenship. Rossant, Sunée, Furiya, and Lin-Liu discuss their frustration at being treated by their interlocutors as crypto-foreigners, or people whose appearance does not match the prevalent ideas about what Americans should look or sound like.

Expatriation and "Local" Foodways

Expatriation figures in three geographic regions in these memoirs: Tanzania, France, and China. Colette Rossant's third volume of her memoirs, *The World in My Kitchen,* recalls how she accompanied her husband Jimmy to Tanzania for his work with the United Nations. There, Rossant draws upon her cosmopolitan background to befriend the locals and obtain the best available local ingredients. Korean American adoptee Kim Sunée is swept off her feet by Olivier Baussan, a French businessman and founder of L'Occitane cosmetics, and moves with him to his estate in the South of France. In *Trail of Crumbs,* she chronicles their life together, and the local food she learns to feed his daughter and their circle of friends. Finally, there are three memoirs about China penned by Asian American women. The first is Japanese American writer Linda Furiya's second volume of her memoirs, *How to Cook a Dragon,* which focuses on the years she spent in mainland China as the trailing spouse of an American businessman. Jen Lin-Liu's two volumes cover her transformation from a freelance journalist, trained and certified Chinese chef, and cooking school owner in *Serve the People* to a food writer and newlywed traveling along the Silk Road in *On the Noodle Road.*

Expatriation privileges the working partner within a romantic relationship by validating that person's presence abroad through his or her professional affiliation. The legal and social status of the nonworking partner is more problematic because it is only through the romantic relationship that he or she finds him- or herself residing outside of the homeland. Trailing spouses are often barred from securing paying positions because of the complications of their legal status; their only "sponsor" is their mate, whereas the partner's residence abroad is legtimized by an actual employer. Thus, nonworking spouses or romantic partners often find themselves relegated to the domestic realm as expatriates, a situation that can challenge the stability of the relationship, especially when the women involved left careers of their own behind. Yet even this division of labor becomes fraught when local customs dictate that foreigners employ local housekeepers or cooks within the household, thereby making the unemployed, trailing spouse feel like a supernumerary presence in both the partner's social circle and within the home. The memoirists discussed in this chapter found themselves facing such a dilemma at one point or another during their stay abroad, and decided to pursue their passion for cooking as both an avocation and the source of their inspiration for other creative pursuits. Learning to prepare local dishes gave these women a way to connect with the history and culture of their homes away from home, and this process also helped them develop transferrable skills they could put to use either in feeding their significant others and their circle of friends or in connecting with other expatriates.

Expatriation is distinctly different from immigration, since the expatriate is not overburdened by the idea or expectation of full assimilation into the adopted culture since his or her stay abroad can always be thought of as temporary, regardless of how long it actually lasts. Expatriates are people willingly displaced from their country of origin, and expressly concerned with the process of negotiating their life abroad as foreign residents, as opposed to tourists, casual visitors, or natives. Professionals working abroad often enjoy an upper-class lifestyle in terms of comforts and luxuries, but they are not in the leisure or the ruling classes where they live. Unlike immigrants, expatriates continue to maintain both legal and affective connections with their birthplace, identifying as citizens of that nation-state even if not physically residing there for many years. Migration historian Nancy L. Green distinguishes between the two different legal categories of "expatriation," the legal process through which a state strips citizenship away from a person, and "emigration," whereby an individual chooses to leave his or her country of origin in order to permanently set up a household someplace else and pledge allegiance to that new nation state. As Green explains, "the concept of expatriation must be understood as both a legal and a social construct," and thus she contends that

> legal debates in the United States over citizenship rights and obligations have been grounded in the political and the social. The shifting image of the presumed expatriate has helped frame the legal issues tackled at each juncture. By laying the basis for an interactive history of the figure of the leave-taker and the state's legislating of citizenship loss, we can see how the "imagined expatriate" has played an important part in constructing the ways in which citizenship has been conceived. (Green 2009, 310)

Expatriation is even more complicated for naturalized citizens. Relatively few individuals choose to expatriate legally by actually giving up their citizenship. Calling oneself an expatriate need not imply a long-lasting commitment to a sole nation-state, merely the decision to live outside of one's country of origin for a period of time longer than the average vacation.

In *Trail of Crumbs, The World in My Kitchen, How to Feed a Dragon, On the Noodle Road,* and *Serve the People,* the writers' status as ethnic American expatriates means that they do not simply idealize the process of reconnecting to an imaginary homeland but instead discuss the difficulties of maintaining an "American" cultural and gastronomic identity that is geographically situated, temporally oriented, and affirmed through contact with other expatriates. These women claim subject positions that place them at the margins of mainstream American society: Asian Americans Sunée, Furiya, and Lin-Liu and Franco-Jewish American Rossant are all part of interracial unions with white men. Their memoirs all ask their readers to contemplate the trials and tribulations of expatriate life from both a culinary and a romantic standpoint. By reading the books or following the recipes, the reading audience becomes transformed into "imagined expatriates" without having to dust off their passports or make travel arrangements. In contrast, the writers' interactions with actual expatriates make them feel excluded and like their American citizenship is not validated.

Colette Rossant, for example, had an easier time befriending and bartering with her Tanzanian neighbors than connecting with the Anglo-American expatriate community: "I made very few friends among the expatriates, who let it be known that they didn't quite approve of my friendship with the Tanzanians and Sikhs. They tended to avoid me because I often talked about my new Tanzanian friends and their children" (Rossant 2006, 159). Her expatriate acquaintances sought to police her performance of whiteness, finding fault in her failure to exercise its privileges, especially since her French-Egyptian origins and American citizenship by marriage made her neither fully one of them nor a racially marked Other. Linda Furiya's second memoir with recipes, *How to Cook a Dragon*, not only recalls her own experience as a Japanese American expatriate living in China with her white American boyfriend, but also discusses at length how different types of expatriate communities function in Chinese cities like Shanghai and Beijing. According to Eric, Furiya's boyfriend, and his expat friends, Americans living in China fall into one of three distinct camps: The first is "the Colonialist White Man," whom they describe as someone primarily interested in "exploiting the economy and the women, living here until the opportunities run dry." Next, "the China Soul is someone who comes innocently enough to China to study the language, but then gets engulfed in the culture" and likely "end[s] up marrying a Chinese woman and never going home." The third and final type of expat these men describe is the xenophobic American who is willfully "living in Denial" by remaining as insulated from Chinese culture and daily life as possible. These people carry on as if they were not in China: "They live on compounds on the outskirts of town that literally look like a neighborhood in the States" (Furiya 2008, 29). Unsurprisingly, the stereotypical expat Furiya's boyfriend and his friends describe is male and employed outside of the home. Though somewhat useful in elucidating the general attitudes of people living abroad toward their country of residence and its people, these broad categories do not really help Furiya learn to negotiate expatriate life in China as a Japanese American woman.

While Jen Lin-Liu's first book, *Serve the People,* saw her diving headlong into Chinese culture, cuisine, and day-to-day life in the traditional *hutong* courtyard housing, by the time she wrote the next volume, *On the Noodle Road,* the thrill of "going native" had worn off:

> Sure, I could pass as a local, with my Asian appearance and the fluency I'd gained in Mandarin. But I remained firmly American, and with my American husband I settled into the lifestyle of many foreigners living overseas. After a period of being enamored with all things local, we'd begun living as if we were back home. We formed friendships with many compatriots, most of whom were journalists, like us. We passed over Chinese newspapers (which censorship had made rote and boring anyway) for *The New York Times* and other American publications. We went to the movies for the latest Hollywood blockbusters. And when it came to food, I was no longer content to eat just Chinese, a cuisine I'd immersed myself in for years. We shopped at a foreign market called Jenny Lou's and dined at new restaurants that served everything from Vietnamese to Spanish to South American, a reflection of how international Beijing had become. (Lin-Liu 2013, 16)

Although she adamantly proclaims her patriotism, Lin-Liu never really specifies which of her particular attributes, views, values, or characteristics (other than her American husband) "firmly" establish her within an American national imaginary. The strident nationalism of this passage is in stark contrast to her later revelation that at an early age she chose to legally change her "given name from Ching-Yee to Jennifer—an indication of my identity struggle" (Lin-Liu 2013, 77). Her marriage to Craig guarantees she enjoys the company of at least one other American expatriate while living abroad; the couple has a network of expatriate friends with whom they socialize, and his parents join them for part of the trek along the Silk Road.

In much the same way that crypto-foreigner, ethnic Americans struggle for acceptance as compatriots by people who cannot see past their physiognomy as an embodied signifier of their race or ethnicity at home, becoming an expatriate can also bring with it a persistent misrecognition of the ethnic American person's claims to national belonging and citizenship status. This dissonance can be either beneficial or detrimental. Asian American memoirists like Jen Lin-Liu, Linda Furiya, and Kim Sunée find themselves subjected to two different types of Orientalizing gazes during their time abroad: Europeans view Kim Sunée as impossibly exotic, inscrutable, and a hypersexualized object of desire simply because of her Korean heritage, while their Chinese interlocutors refuse to see any difference between themselves and Jen Lin-Liu and Linda Furiya, insisting upon their Chinese-ness even when the women's heritage is from elsewhere in Asia. Sunée is constantly dismissed by her French boyfriend's neighbors and acquaintances as "that *chinoise* Olivier has taken up with" (Sunée 2008, xviii). Even when potential suitors acknowledge her nationality as American, they nonetheless insist upon Orientalizing Kim: "Allez, don't be so *américaine,* my little Asian flower" (Sunée 2008, 264). Sunée is eternally perceived as a crypto-foreigner, an outsider both to mainstream French society and to the United States; her Asian features are a constant reminder of that country's colonial past, while her American-ness is inherent in her refusal to conflate business (working as an English tutor) with pleasure (becoming the student's mistress). In *How To Cook a Dragon,* Linda Furiya explains that as a Japanese American woman in China, she feels isolated, not quite recognized as "American" by the Chinese nationals, who assume she is either a Japanese national in China for business, or else a Chinese gold-digger specializing in dating rich Americans, a situation similar to the disdain Kim Sunée and Olivier endured when they went out in public in South Korea. Though all of these writers discuss some aspects of family life marked by the family experience of immigration, such as growing up bilingual or traveling to the ancestral homeland, they faced different levels of discrimination and prejudice depending on their ability to physically blend in with the dominant society both at home and abroad.

Memoirists as Romantic Heroines Who Cook

The romance narrative structure of the memoirs adds a level of intrigue or piquancy to otherwise straightforward tales of living and cooking abroad. Although romantic relationships and professional dilemmas are at the core of these immigrant expat memoirs with recipes, these texts are more than mere formulaic, chick-lit accounts of self-improvement and finding love abroad during one well-compensated year of travelling, á la Elizabeth Gilbert's best seller, *Eat, Pray, Love.* Kim Sunée, Colette Rossant, Linda Furiya, and Jen Lin-Liu all strive to balance the competing demands of using cooking to sustain their respective romantic relationships while also drawing inspiration from the kitchen to develop or reclaim their own narrative voices as writers. Their texts appeal to female readers by aligning the descriptions of their experiences abroad within the familiar genre conventions of romance fiction: girl meets boy, girl and boy fall in love, girl and boy move to another country, and chaos ensues within their relationship. Though they are food-themed female empowerment narratives, the memoirs prominently chronicle the highs and lows of each woman's romantic life. Thus, the pleasures readers derive from reading women discussing their love lives in food memoirs with recipes parallel those enjoyed by readers of romance fiction narratives, as Kristin Ramsdell outlines in *Romance Fiction: A Guide to the Genre*. The expatriate memoir and romance fiction overlap in yet another way: their shared emphasis on real-world challenges and problems that women face as they struggle to determine how to care for others and fulfill their own desires. Ramsdell points out that readers of romance fiction expect their heroines to face many obstacles on their way to romantic bliss, and that the correspondence between those problems and actual social ills enhances the pleasure they derive from their reading:

> Romances also deal with important life changes and social issues, both inevitable and unexpected, such as aging, pregnancy, abandonment, spousal and child abuse, divorce, death, grief, alcoholism, racism, prejudice of all kinds, and mental and physical illness. While this might not seem to be appealing on the surface, it speaks to the needs of a great many readers; it allows them not only to confront real-world problems through fiction, but also to envision healthy, hopeful, and successful solutions and outcomes. (Ramsdell 1999, 23)

Readers of these ethnic expat memoirs with recipes encounter first-person accounts of abortion, divorce, adopted child syndrome, sexism, single parenting, the glass ceiling, and pervasive poverty in developing countries; the memoirs also contain hard lessons about state-sponsored violence through references to the Vichy occupation of France and the purges of the Cultural Revolution in China, the omnipresent surveillance of life in modern-day Iran, alcoholism, and persecution of racial, ethnic, or religious minorities.

Tanzania

Colette Rossant has come full circle in her own experience of the American culinary landscape. At the twilight of her life, she looks back on her youthful ideas about the United States, framed, quite appropriately, by books: "I remembered reading a book written by two French journalists about their travels in America. I must have been sixteen when I read it. I was fascinated with the authors' tales of New York, the Rocky Mountains, California, and ice cream sundaes" (Rossant 2006, 11). While the iconic dessert inevitably disappointed Rossant once she tried it in New York, where she and her new husband, Jimmy, had settled, it nonetheless represented all of her hopes and desires for what life would be like in this new country, as she recalls: "Could I tell Jimmy that for years America for me was defined by an ice-cream sundae? Never!" (Rossant 2006, 11). This passage is an instance where Colette Rossant deploys the joint narrative subject position of the "coupled-self"; even in articulating her own food cravings, as a narrator Rossant nonetheless invokes Jimmy's imagined approval or dismissal, thereby triangulating the discussion of food away from her as a desiring individual toward them as a couple. Despite this disclaimer, Rossant's realization about food's power to convey a sense of national identity proves useful later on when she, Jimmy, and their youngest child, Thomas, spend some time in Tanzania.

While Jimmy was hard at work drawing the plans for what would become the new Tanzanian capital of Dodoma, Colette Rossant and her teenaged son, Thomas, who had taught himself to speak Swahili, braved the local markets in search of food to prepare in their rudimentary charcoal stove, since access to electricity was unpredictable. After a visit to the local butcher revealed nothing but flies-strewn "chunks . . . of goat and beef" (Rossant 2006, 154), Rossant decided to take matters into her own hands. She approached a small-scale butcher who operated during the Saturday market, Philip, and made a business proposition: "I proposed a plan that would benefit us both: I'd teach him how to butcher the goats the European way, and he would gain expatriate clients willing to pay a much higher price for the meat" (Rossant 2006, 155). While at first glance this exchange might appear merely paternalistic—an arrogant European proposing to teach a native African the "proper" way to do what he's been doing all his life—I offer a more nuanced reading. Rossant's business proposal drew on her personal experience as a European/American expatriate and her professional expertise as a cookbook writer and cooking teacher (though her butchering skills were the result of book learning derived from her reading of Fanny Farmer's cookbook, rather than a formal culinary training). Also, she did not exploit Philip to suit her needs; instead, she actively leveraged her expat social network for his benefit by personally canvassing all the expat residences she knew to inform them about the new European-style butcher offering goat meat in familiar cuts at the Saturday market. As someone who knew firsthand the power of iconic (or at least familiar) food to conjure up visceral memories of specific geographical locales (the sundae version of America, a sirloin conjuring up visions of home), Rossant effectively tapped into the "imagined expat" gustatory imaginary and helped a local man establish a thriving and sustainable business.

None of the recipes contained in *The World in My Kitchen* are identifiably Tanzanian, perhaps because Rossant encountered such difficulties acquiring staple food items other than Philip's goats. She and Thomas enjoyed the experience of working together to make themselves understood in Swahili, and to learn about local cultures, including the Masai—with whom they had trouble overcoming the linguistic barrier—and the Wagogos, who spoke Swahili. This part of the narrative deploys a coupled-self dynamic distinctly different from the Colette/Jimmy pairing prevalent throughout most of Rossant's three food memoirs with recipes. Here, it's the mother-son couple who function as a team, especially since Rossant depends on the intervention of her young and Swahili-fluent son, Thomas, to succeed in establishing the very interpersonal connections she so cherishes. Tanzania holds a special emotional appeal for Rossant and her son: "To this day, I miss Tanzania. I was bitten by the African bug. I loved the country and its people. I had made many friends, and from afar, followed their lives, hoping that one day I would return" (Rossant 2006, 164–65). Rossant did not exploit the affective ties that bind her to that community by profiting from what she learned about their cuisine and turning it into a cookbook. Instead, the expat experience in Tanzania prompted Rossant to channel her newfound interest into learning more about different cultures and countries around the world.

France

Sunée's book offers a mix of rustic dishes from three regions in the global South: the Provence region in the South of France, her South Korean birthplace, and the American South, figured by her Louisiana upbringing. Although the majority of the memoir chronicles her time in France, the larger pattern of Sunée's life is a series of wanderings through multiple public markets, perhaps signaling to her need to recreate the circumstances surrounding the initial trauma of being abandoned by her Korean mother. She looks to food, and her own eating habits and preferences, as a way of maintaining a personal history of the woman she is evolving into: "Over the years, I've also kept tasting notes, menus, and jotted-down recipes, clues as to what I crave that may help me to know who I am, better understand how food has the power to ground and comfort in times of disarray" (Sunée 2008, 61). The recipes in the book mark these different stages in her eating and cooking life, thus giving readers glimpses of how specific dishes encapsulate certain chapters in her personal evolution. Throughout, Sunée cultivates three distinct relational cooking identities: the childhood memories of cooking alongside her grandfather Poppy in New Orleans; the intimate family moments where she prepared food for her boyfriend, Olivier, and his daughter, Laure, as well as their joint friends and acquaintances in the South of France; and, finally, the comfort food the newly single Sunée eats in Paris after their breakup.

Lacking a clear family history, but haunted by shadowy memories of a brother and grandmother in Korea, Sunée becomes keenly aware of how others perceive her and try to assign an exotic or hybrid identity to her physical features. When she meets Madame Song, the woman who will teach her Korean in preparation for the trip she takes to her birthplace with Olivier, Sunée is stunned at the reaction her face inspires. Although Madame Song is familiar with her circumstances, her suggestion that Kim Sunée may be of mixed parentage rather than "pure Korean" challenges Kim's assumptions about herself, her origins, and how she reads to people. Madame Song tried to mend the emotional wound she had inadvertently inflicted by offering to give Sunée the recipe for an authentically Korean dish: *bi-bim-bap*. Tellingly, the recipe for this dish is not included in the memoir, thereby underscoring Sunée's feeling that her Korean-ness is inauthentic due to her status as an American adoptee. When Kim and Olivier arrived in Korea some months later, almost no one brought up the issue of her potential mixed parentage. Instead, the couple was denied service at fine eating establishments because people assumed Sunée was a prostitute keeping the rich European man company.[1] This misunderstanding of the couple's status confirmed Sunée's sense that those with whom she interacts see her only as the embodiment of an Oriental stereotype, rather than as an individual. These musings extend even to her insecurity about Olivier, and come to a head after she overheard a heated exchange between her lover and his estranged wife: "'*Chintok*,' I whisper to myself when Olivier has left the room. Chink. Gook. Sounds of words that become swords. To Dominique I am an object, for Olivier, a treasure. A precious chinoiserie" (Sunée 2008, 95; emphasis original). Thus, despite Sunée's love for Olivier and her acculturation to French and Provençal culture, her deep insecurity about his attraction to her remained a problem that was never fully resolved. Further marking her isolation and sense of doubt is the fact that Sunée did not come

---

1. This situation parallels how the local Chinese people had dismissed Furiya and Eric in *How to Cook a Dragon*.

into contact with many other American expats in the social circles in which she and Baussan moved, thus making her the sole representative of multiple and, to other people, irreconcilable subject positions (American, Korean, Chinese?) at once.

Unlike most of the writers who preceded her and who had a firm understanding of their socially proscribed roles within both the fabric of the American nation and the more narrow social circles they left behind, Sunée spends the bulk of her memoir with recipes grappling with the problem of what it means to be "American" since this was not a nationality into which she was born, but rather, was adopted into. Even the book's title, *Trail of Crumbs*, a clear reference to the mechanism the young abandoned siblings futilely devise to find their way back home from the dark forest where their weak father and evil stepmother abandoned them in the fairy tale *Hansel and Gretel*, alludes to the pervasive sense of displacement that suffuses the memoir. Whereas birds eat the breadcrumbs the children scatter on their second forced journey into the forest, leaving them stranded and eager to take shelter in a bewitched candy house, in this memoir readers occupy the bird role, following along the narrative path Sunée sets out for them, consuming tidbits about her actual abandonment as a toddler in a Korean food market where her mother left her when she was three years old. Like the fairy tale's titular children, Sunée has to become self-reliant in order to break free from her own tempting "candy house" prison: France.

Sunée's fascination with France subsides after the breakup of her three-year partnership with Olivier Baussan. She chronicles the various stages in their courtship and romance through descriptions of food and how they relate to one another in the kitchen. A disastrous Christmas dinner, where Sunée burned the main course and Olivier angrily took over, only to undercook the potatoes and oversalt the fish, epitomizes the anger and resentment of their fraying romance, and soon after Sunée moved out for good. Through it all, however, Sunée refers to Olivier as her primary point of reference—would he have enjoyed this meal? Does he typically eat or avoid these ingredients? These considerations are present even when the meals she discusses are prepared for other men, thereby attesting to the primacy of this coupled-self as a narrative constant throughout the memoir.

Whereas Hansel and Gretel foiled the cannibalistic witch's plan to eat them by taking control of their desires for candy and not eating to the point of making their bodies appear more "juicy," "plump," or "delicious" to the would-be cook in the fairy tale, Sunée's grief over the loss of love likewise manifested itself as a loss of appetite, making her feel less appealing to other men. Upon returning to France from South America, where she and the last fling discussed in the memoir had vacationed, Sunée found that she had entirely lost her appetite. Forewarnings of this may have been evident even during the trip itself, from which Sunée shared only three somewhat generic pasta recipes, which are in the order of mere variations on a theme: "Midnight Pasta Three Ways" (Sunée 2008, 361). Ironically, even the casual references Sunée makes to the lackluster meals she forces herself to eat at this point in her life are designed to make American readers' mouths water. She summed up her routine as primarily a regimen of "eating mostly small spoonfuls of yogurt late in the night, a few slices of salted tomatoes, and stale *pain au chocolat*" with an occasional break: "Sometimes I make myself eat a hot ham-and-Gruyere crepe from an early morning street vendor" (Sunée 2008, 367). These episodes dealing with her sudden lack of appetite exemplify how Sunée coped with her feelings of loss and abandonment as a child. By describing these meals in lush, though not overly long detail, Sunée the narrator involves the reader in this triangulated chain of desire, both for the simple foods of one's childhood—yogurt and grilled cheese sandwiches—but also for their exotic French doppelgangers: French yogurt, grilled crepes with gooey French cheese. It is not until she finally decided to move back to the United States that her appetite returned, but her American readers have already been salivating over the simple comfort foods she had been enjoying.

Kim Sunée most fully inhabits or performs her American citizenship when she declares in the closing pages of her memoir: "I have learned that home is in my heart—in all the places and people I have left behind. It's in the food that I cook and share with others, in the cities I will come to know, and in the offerings of street vendors around the world—from South Korea to Provence—in the markets I have yet to discover" (Sunée 2008, 369). The imagined community of which she sees herself a part is a transnational network of food vendors and home cooks, all bound together by a hungry group of friends. Ultimately, though, *Trail of Crumbs* fulfills this home function most clearly because through the book Sunée actually "share[s] with others" food in cities across the globe, whether she has physically been there or not.

China

Despite the didacticism implicit in its title, *How to Cook a Dragon*, Linda Furiya's memoir begins with her speaking as an eater or consumer of Chinese cuisine, rather than from the more authoritative subject position of the experienced cook who has mastered any of its regional specialties. Linda Furiya's first reference to food in *How to Cook a Dragon* depicts her as a neophyte learning the proper way to eat Beijing duck from her boyfriend:

> I watched as Eric smeared the steamy pancake with the dark plum sauce. He added a couple of slices of scallion and a sliver of duck meat, topped with the skin. He rolled the pancake up tight, and I waited for him to sink his teeth into the juicy roll; instead, he handed it to me, and I didn't hesitate to grab it.
>
> All those centuries of work came together in that first perfect bite. There was nothing I could think of that compared with the smoky duck meat mingling with the sweet plum sauce and clean, piquant scallion. I ate it in two bites. (Furiya 2008, 11)

Eric's genteel gesture of handing the roll to Furiya instead of eating it himself attests to his good manners and suave demeanor, but also can be read metaphorically as modeling the behavior that will help Linda fit in with this "foreign" society. This passage illustrates two themes that recur throughout the rest of the book. The first is dependency, since the entire length of her stay in China is mediated through Furiya's relationship with Eric, whose familiarity with the culture and mastery of Mandarin made him the insider. Because of the language barrier, Furiya only has access to mediated cultural experiences—such as Mandarin lessons and cooking classes for expatriates. Thus, she does not fret overmuch about vouching for the "traditional" nature of the recipes she offers. The second theme is authenticity, because Furiya learned to prepare the dishes whose recipes she includes in the memoir both from Chinese *ayis*, the professional housekeepers/cooks who work for expatriates, and the local staff at the Chinese cooking school Linda attended while working for an expat magazine. But it was precisely her affiliation with such a publication, and by extension with the audience who reads it, that marks her inability to fully fit in with local society and, ultimately, with Eric's lifestyle.

Linda befriended a series of American expatriate women. Whenever she introduces them, Linda describes both their physical appearance and marital status, thereby conveying that her world view is clearly one in which people exist as part of romantic couples or "coupled selves." Furiya met these women in connection with the expat magazine for which she wrote about food. The first is Susan, the editor, "a Caucasian woman in her early forties, dressed in a well-worn navy blue Mao suit and looking very much like a young girl except for her chin-length, prematurely gray hair" (Furiya 2008, 79). Susan was married to a Chinese man and they had children together. The next woman is Gina, who worked in the advertisement department. A fellow San Francisco transplant like Furiya, Gina was "half-Chinese, half-Caucasian" (Furiya 2008, 83), and she also had become an expat due to her husband's professional ambitions, though in Gina's case this situation led her to become the family's breadwinner. "I learned that Gina's Korean American husband had brought her to Beijing when he'd decided he wanted to master the language. He was studying full-time and she needed to work, which is why she'd come on board to help Susan" (Furiya 2008, 83–84). Interacting with these women helped Linda feel more grounded in China; having a group of girlfriends allowed her to affirm who she was. Unfortunately, she took this newfound confidence and feminist affirmation and infused it into her interactions with students in her Mandarin classes, some of whom, like the Chinese couple from Indonesia, Rudi and Inga, were in China to reconnect with their heritage after growing up in the diaspora. Upon learning from Inga that Rudi did not really value this heritage trip and was eager to return home, Furiya advises her to go it alone, and the couple broke up. In recounting this episode, Furiya is quick to convey a knowing sense of how hypocritical this advice was, given how shaky her own relationship with Eric was. However, flush with a sense of female empowerment and sisterly validation, Furiya quieted her own doubts and plowed ahead, suppressing the gnawing feeling that "Inga, like Julie and Joe, and eventually even us, would become just another casualty of the transient Beijing expatriate culture" (Furiya 2008, 101). Although Eric had wooed Linda Furiya with the promise that living abroad together would strengthen their fragile bond, she feared that her linguistic isolation, coupled with the artificial dependence on him which the situation imposes upon her, would actually drive them apart, which it eventually did.

Linda Furiya's two pregnancies were what finally pushed the couple to the breaking point. The first time around, Linda and Eric were not married, and they worried about what childbirth in China would be like. They decided upon an abortion, waiting to start their family until they and their relationship were more settled. A recipe for "Tender Chicken Breasts with Firecracker Sauce" (Furiya 2008, 172) follows this traumatic episode in her life, the spiciness of the sauce a metaphor for the release she feels that recounting her experience has had on the memory of the child she did not have. A few years later, Linda and Eric did marry, but made plans to return to the United States for the delivery of the child they decided to carry to term. The question about where to raise their child was what finally undid their marriage: Eric wanted to remain in Shanghai but Linda called for a return to the States. There is no recipe after the epilogue that conveys the news of their divorce not long after their son's birth. Instead, Furiya closes the memoir with a quick reference to the last visits she made to her favorite Shanghai restaurants before leaving for the States: "I lingered over each meal, savoring them like a farewell kiss. Most of those dishes I could never re-create, nor would I ever want to attempt making. I was confident that I would return someday, but I knew it wouldn't be soon" (Furiya 2008, 315). This is an ironic way to end a memoir with recipes, because it teases readers with culinary delights unavailable to them and to Furiya. Despite the unhappy end to the love story, Furiya's memoir reassures the reader that she can nourish her son and provide for his well-being now that she has mastered some aspects of Chinese cuisine and found her voice as a writer.

Jen Lin-Liu's second memoir, *On the Noodle Road*, likewise closes with a happy announcement of her pregnancy and the couple's indecision about where to settle down as a new family. However, the tone throughout this and her debut memoir, *Serve the People*, is less gloomy, more confident of her ability to handle any circumstance than is the tone of either *How to Cook a Dragon* or *Trail of Crumbs*. Lin-Liu's can-do pluckiness and her willingness to follow her stomach in search of a good meal recall Colette Rossant's similar qualities, chronicled in *The World in My Kitchen*. Unlike the rest of the women whose work I examine in this chapter, Lin-Liu chose to become an expatriate in Beijing long before she met and fell in love with Craig, her husband. Although by the end of her first memoir she has achieved her twin goals of becoming both a food journalist and a trained chef certified by the Chinese national exam, she also concludes her account by announcing her engagement, thereby recasting the entire tale of her culinary adventure as a fairy-tale romance.

In *Serve the People*, Lin-Liu puts her Chinese American heritage and her travel journalism background to use as she guides readers through Chinese history writ large across both the countryside and the urban landscape. Jen took her interest in food seriously, enrolling in, and graduating from, a local professional cooking school, apprenticing in a variety of Chinese restaurant kitchens, and finally setting up her very own cooking school and restaurant in Beijing, Black Sesame Kitchen, that employed the very people who first taught her to cook. However, when she first got serious about learning to cook, she realized just how rudimentary her approach to cooking had been:

> My culinary skills had been limited to making basics like pasta and stir-fries, and baking cookies and brownies—out of a box. When I was growing up, cooking had never been emphasized at home, since I was supposed to

become a doctor or a lawyer, and my years in China hadn't improved my culinary skills, since eating out was so cheap and easy. (Lin-Liu 2008, 27)

By sharing her own inexperience and ignorance of proper techniques and the wide range of local ingredients, Lin-Liu sets the stage for her American readers to overcome their own qualms and try the recipes contained within the volume. This passage constitutes yet another way through which Lin-Liu performs her American-ness through the narrator function of the memoir—by having been brought up to focus on a career rather than being expected to master the domestic arts in preparation for an early marriage. Besides her entrepreneurial efforts, Lin-Liu had a series of steady gigs working as a freelance reporter for an American magazine, and later as the editor of the English-language version of *Time Out Beijing*, a cultural magazine. These jobs helped Jen finance her passion for cooking as well as her trips throughout China.

Like Sunée who communicated easily in French while in Provence Lin-Liu was fluent in the local language by the time she sets up house in China, so she had a more immediate and "authentic" engagement with the locals than Furiya ever could. However, whereas Furiya had already undergone the process of claiming an ethnic identity as a Japanese American woman that was markedly different from that of her immigrant parents by the time she moved to China with Eric, Jen Lin-Liu grappled with her ethnicity and its implications only after deciding to relocate there for work. She recalls: "I straddled the expatriate bubble and the Chinese world outside it, not quite belonging to either. So it was in China, ironically, that for the first time I felt the urge to call myself a Chinese American. It was the first time I had to seriously grapple with issues of race, identity, and where I fit in" (Lin-Liu 2008, 18). Despite this new ethnic consciousness, all three Asian American women experienced the double burden of being regarded with suspicion in Asia for not quite fitting in with people's expectations of what either "Americans" or "Asians" look like. Jen faced rejection from both Chinese nationals and Western expatriates, and the frustration she felt with her lack of intelligibility comes through in the following passage:

> I was weary of arriving at meetings to be greeted by people demanding to know where "the American" was to whom they had spoken on the phone. I was tired of Chinese security guards detaining me at the gates of foreign diplomatic compounds, unconvinced that I was going to visit friends until I produced my passport, while more obvious foreigners breezed through. I

was sick of people wondering why I spoke Mandarin with a funny accent and why I didn't understand the idioms. (Lin-Liu 2008, 17–18)

By mastering the art of Chinese cooking, so to speak, Lin-Liu altered the nature of her encounters with others. She presented herself to Chinese cooking professionals as a neophyte in need of guidance, and as she gradually acquired more skills and apprenticed herself to professional noodle makers and fine restaurateurs alike, she mastered a language all can understand: food. This was the cultural capital that gave her currency with both locals and her compatriots. Culinary skill translates across cultures and can obviate a language barrier. Becoming both a foodie and a certified chef made Lin-Liu legible to multiple audiences.

On the Noodle Road begins after Lin-Liu's wedding, as she undertakes her first major research project in pursuit of two mysteries: How did noodles as a foodstuff spread from Asia to Europe? And, more immediately relevant to her life as a newlywed, how do women around the world adjust to their role as "wives"? What lends the book its suspense is not the competing claims for the noodle's origins in either China or Italy, but instead, the question of whether Lin-Liu's feminist need to assert her independence from her husband and maintain her professional identity would doom the marriage before the journey ended. As she traveled to multiple countries along the Silk Road in her quest to find the mythic origins of the noodle, she reported that few people seemed as troubled by her claim to an American identity as they are about the absence of her husband or her lack of children. In these contexts, Lin-Liu's gender, figured both physically, through having to cover her head while visiting Muslim territories, and culturally, by her expressed interest in the domestic art of cookery, marked her as more of an "outsider" to her local interlocutors, whether male or female, than did the nationality stamped on her passport.

Whereas Furiya's and Sunée's memoirs focus on the outward manifestation of the interpersonal aspects of their relationships with their beloved—such as arguments, tone of voice, or word choice—even after things go awry, Lin-Liu's worries about her ability to maintain her own independence while being a supportive partner to Craig are conveyed as first-person singular narrative in her second book rather than imputing any specific motive to his actions or comments. She tells the reader directly that Craig felt uncomfortable about her depiction of him in *Serve the People*, and thus she consciously avoided relying too heavily on the "coupled-self" narrative construction. However, he did play a more active role in the journey that Lin-Liu chronicles in *On the Noodle Road,* which turns out to be a more conventional travel account than her first tome. Craig escorted Lin-Liu through Kyrgyzstan, Uzbekistan, Turkmenistan, and Iran, and showed up again as his schedule permitted, finally rejoining Jen at the tail end of her travels in Italy. Their marriage emerged stronger for being tested by distance and professional ambition. What most surprised Jen when she and her husband reunited at journey's end was that he had taken an interest in cooking. Along the Silk Road, the couple had taken a couple of detours so that Craig could enjoy hiking, a sport about which he was passionate. When he returned the favor by learning to cook, Lin-Liu was flattered and surprised that he had begun his own culinary evolution. Structurally, Craig's newly developed kitchen chops stand in for those of the readers who have followed the recipes in both volumes of Lin-Liu's memoirs and have thus, presumably, improved their own kitchen skills.

Although Jen Lin-Liu, Linda Furiya, Kim Sunée, Colette Rossant lived as expatriates at different time periods and in different corners of the globe, their memoirs with recipes all contribute to an ongoing dialogue about race, ethnicity, and belonging to an American imagined community of professional women who make their living by writing about food and cooking. Their tales of romance enhance the sense of adventure the memoirs convey, despite the fact that the majority of the events each woman describes have to do with the mundane details of setting up a household in a foreign land. Discussions of linguistic mastery and acculturation highlight the difficulties inherent in adapting to life in a foreign country, whether that experience is part of temporary expatriation or of permanent immigration. Reading about these women's firsthand difficulties with language and unfamiliar customs should, theoretically, prompt readers to be more empathetic when encountering immigrants having similar difficulties fitting into American life. Finally, through their shared emphasis on the cultural (and linguistic) ties and privileges that all American citizens (whether born, adopted, or naturalized) have access to, *Trail of Crumbs, The World in My Kitchen, How to Cook a Dragon, Serve the People,* and *On the Noodle Road* emerge as unpretentious feminist manifestoes.

Chapter 5

Diasporic Inventions
Reclaiming Family Culinary Traditions

Few times of the year are as emotionally fraught and gastronomically demanding for individuals, families, and their friends as are holidays with religious overtones. In this chapter, I argue that children and grandchildren of immigrants feel compelled to identify more closely with their family heritage through the ritual preparation and consumption of family recipes tied to either an originary homeland, like Africa, or to a distinct cultural or religious tradition, such as Judaism. This move to reclaim a diasporic tradition that is otherwise forgotten or discarded throughout most of the year is not merely the result of an affected nostalgia for an idealized homeland, nor is it simply a belated rejection of the immigrant family's assimilation to a dominant American white and secular society. Instead, the memoirs discussed in this chapter detail the writers' purposeful reclamation of a meaningful relationship to the past mediated through their participation in food-based rituals that fit the general profile of what Marxist historian Eric Hobsbawm, himself a Jewish immigrant, discusses in *The Invention of Tradition*: "'Invented tradition' is taken to mean a set of practices, normally governed by overtly or tacitly accepted rules and of a ritual or symbolic nature, which seek to inculcate certain values and norms of behavior by repetition, which automatically implies continuity with the past" (Hobsbawm and Ranger 2013, 1). It is this desire to maintain a "continuity with the past," an affective connection that transcends the physical dislocation through geographical dispersal, that drives immigrants, their children, and/or their grandchildren to reclaim, invent, or customize traditions tied to their personal background in order to imbue their lives in America with a deeper sense of purpose and of rootedness. As postcolonial studies scholar Betty Joseph remarks, this tailoring of the idea of an ancestral homeland to suit one's desire for a meaningful heritage is characteristic of this era of technological connectedness and social networking: "what we are seeing now is diasporics who shrink and expand this place of origin and activate several different identities that are not continuous with those of the nation-state" (Joseph 2012, 211). Although Joseph's comments were made in the context of her discussion of Indian expatriates, this chapter will discuss how other contemporary "diasporics," members of the African, Jewish, and even Soviet diasporas, recount their decision to reclaim rituals or traditions they did not grow up appreciating or even practicing. Here I turn to two distinct but related archives—memoirs with recipes and how-to manuals for celebrating these invented diasporic traditions (in Hobsbsawm's terms)—to contrast the performative opportunities each offers.

The works under discussion in this chapter chronicle the writers' decision to embark upon a combined genealogical and gastronomic undertaking by celebrating specific cultural traditions through family recipes. Elizabeth Ehrlich's *Miriam's Kitchen: A Memoir,* Ntozake Shange's *If I Can Cook / You Know God Can,* and Anya Von Bremzen's *Mastering the Art of Soviet Cooking: A Memoir of Food and Longing* all exemplify the desire to enrich their own experience of being hyphenated Americans by preserving and passing on an embodied performance of cultural belonging in a transnational or diasporic context. Ehrlich, Shange, and Von Bremzen frame their discussions of specific meals or recipes to represent or highlight their respective families' participation in a set of diasporic practices that constitute a transnational affiliation. The second set of texts examined in this chapter also combine recipes and autobiographical elements, but they may be best understood according to their primary function: to serve as guides or introductions to syncretic rituals involving food that bring together aspects of different traditions and historical contexts invested with personal meaning by those who practice them—like Passover Seders, Kwanzaa, and even Festivus, as I will explain. Jonathan Safran Foer's *New American Haggadah,* Eric V. Copage's *Kwanzaa: An African American Celebration of Culture and Cooking,* and Dan O'Keefe's *The Real Festivus: The True Story Behind America's Favorite Made-Up Holiday* depend for their success upon being accepted and adopted by many into their own family celebrations, and passed down to future generations.

Through a comparative analysis of the memoirs' and manuals' contrasting rhetorical strategies for describing ritual holiday meals, I will explain how these writers negotiate the tension between the authenticity or invented status of the ritual described and the readers' need for guidance in the proper performance of the same.

Displacement as Root Cause of Diasporic Practices

The writers discussed here deploy a diasporic consciousness as a rhetorical strategy to reassert a sense of rootedness in the place where they live, something that does not preclude them from forging ongoing affective and/or cultural connections with a different place or cultural tradition that symbolizes the concept of "home" to them, as anthropologist James Clifford explains in *Routes*:

> The language of diaspora is increasingly invoked by displaced peoples who feel (maintain, revive, invent) a connection with a prior home. This sense of connection must be strong enough to resist erasure through the normalizing processes of forgetting, assimilating, and distancing. Many minority groups that have not previously identified in this way are now reclaiming diasporic origins and affiliations. (Clifford 1997, 255)

Clifford, like Hobsbawm and Joseph, allows for the invented nature of traditions. The renewed interest in minoritarian identification with diaspora communities may be borne out of two diametrically opposed impulses: either it stems from the minority person's inability to fully blend into or gain acceptance by the dominant culture of the country to which his or her family has immigrated or been brought (as in the case of African Americans whose ancestors arrived in this country as slaves via the Middle Passage), or else the minority person develops a new interest in reclaiming his or her family's lost cultural heritage as a conscious disavowal of the community's almost absolute assimilation into mainstream culture. Displacement, in Clifford's view, does not have to be experienced recently, as in the case of minority groups who suddenly wish to claim diasporic identities; it can be a more subtle realization of feeling distant or no longer included in cultural practices closely associated with their specific heritage.

Clifford seeks to find common ground between the two experiences of diaspora he discusses—that borne out of displacement or minority status—by further refining his operational definition of "diaspora": "When understood as a practice of dwelling (differently), as an ambivalent refusal or indefinite deferral of return, and as a positive transnationalism, diaspora finds validation in the historical experiences of both displaced Africans and Jews" (Clifford 1997, 269). Casting diaspora as a "positive" experience of transnationalism, the works under discussion embrace their transnational connections, and the writers enhance their sense of connection to an active, and dynamic, diaspora community. This definition is by no means value-neutral, and Clifford is quick to explain that the emphasis on diaspora as an experience of "dwelling" privileges feminine experiences of diaspora as a permanent way of living in relation to the past over more male perceptions of diaspora as temporary condition that will end at some future time when they return to the homeland.[1] However, since the memoirs analyzed in this section were all published by women and the men penned the how-to handbooks, this combined archive presents a balanced overview of the appeal of invented traditions to both diasporic individuals and the communities to which they want to belong.

Food Writing and Its Performative Functions

Anthropologist Stephan Palmié proposes the concept of "gastrographical revisionism" to describe purposeful rewritings of a culinary event or tradition to fit into larger narratives of national (or religious) belonging. Palmié's comments specifically refer to the development of a cookbook subgenre that chronicles the rise of Afrocentric cooking practices as a culinary heritage distinct from other regional American foodways, but he notes that this trend is part of "a larger heritage industry catering to consumers economically capacitated to engage in a nutritional identity politics of a culinary self-authentication" (Palmié 2009, 56). While tracing the rise of the corporate heritage industry is a productive lens through which to examine the changing landscape of African American cookbook publishing in the United States, I want to apply Palmié's more narrow concept of "gastrographical revisionism" as a theoretical tool to analyze a more deracinated set of cultural practices that still falls under the category of "culinary

---

1. In his discussion of the gendered experiences of diaspora, Clifford refers to the essay "Diaspora: Generation and the Ground of Jewish Identity," written by Daniel Boyarin and Jonathan Boyarin, who propose a model of kinship not based on race, and explicitly point to women's distinct contributions to diasporic Judaism. See Clifford 1997, 270–72.

self-authentication" through their nutritional choices: reclaimed diasporic food rituals that become imbued with the power of heritability, especially when devised and observed within the domestic sphere of the nuclear family unit. Following Joseph and Clifford, I read the six texts discussed here as "diasporic" because they reclaim or invest (or even invent, as per Hobsbawm) existing food-centered rituals with new personal significance through the use of food writing ("gastrography," in Palmié's terms). Writing about these traditions in their respective memoirs enhances the authors' perception of their family's heritage as a rich and meaningful connection to the past.

I want to focus more attention on the first term of this concept, "*gastrographical* revisionism" (my emphasis), to argue that food memoirs with recipes and how-to manuals for food-centered rituals or traditions both emphasize the performative aspect of food writing as a means of (re)enacting the embodied cultural practices of cooking and eating associated with the diasporic traditions in which they partake. In short, what this group of texts focuses on is how people perform ritual and how best to use writing to either describe this performance (memoirs) or else write it into being through performative utterances (manuals).

The three memoirs mentioned earlier discuss small-scale family performances of diasporic rituals with roots in distinctly national culinary traditions—like keeping a kosher kitchen (Jewish), adding mayonnaise to everything (Soviet/Russian), or adopting Caribbean or African ingredients and cooking techniques (Afrocentric). Both memoirs and manuals share the personal significance of these rituals for the people who have chosen to embrace them anew; the way in which each family customizes or tailors these performances of diasporic belonging may put them at odds with the cultural or religious significance out of which the same traditions grew, but at least they are all engaged in similar acts of commemoration. By reading the manuals and memoirs alongside one another, this chapter suggests that the invention of culinary traditions is one way through which diasporic community formation is affirmed. Regardless of whether they originated as religious observances (the Seder and *kahsrut*), cultural expressions of separatist black nationalism (Kwanzaa or feminist pan-Africanism), or as a minor anticonsumerist plot point in a television sitcom or Marxist ideology (Festivus or Soviet propaganda), the food narratives under discussion here all privilege the domestic sphere as the space within which the emotional debt involved in the performance of these diasporic heritage traditions is repaid through the preparation and consumption of family meals.

Reclaiming Jewish Ritual in a Secular Context

In the introduction to *Miriam's Kitchen,* Ehrlich situates herself as an immigrant's daughter (her mother is Canadian), the granddaughter of immigrants (both grandmothers hail from Poland), and the daughter-in-law of Holocaust survivors (Miriam and her father). To this list, we could add immigrant's wife, since her husband was born in Israel and relocated to the United States with his parents as a child. As a convert to *kashrut* (keeping kosher), if not necessarily to the faith of Judaism, Ehrlich reclaimed the cultural heritage her own parents put aside in favor of their more intellectual pursuits. She self-consciously created a Jewish "collage" of invented traditions that both please her and will serve as her legacy:

> The cadence is evolving for me now, as I seek to bring tradition home. With ambivalence and some sense of irony, I light a candle, recite a prayer, grate a potato, and move toward making my kitchen kosher. Thus, I forge links from my grandparents, and my husband's grandparents, to my children, who wear their ancestors' Hebrew names.
>
> I think about it as I go, from a sinkside, stoveside, personal perspective, not a rabbinical one. I turn over the old stories in my mind and collect new ones. I choose my own history, deciding which snapshots, decades, recipes, versions of arguments and events are to be discarded, and which will stand for the whole. That history is my own little temple where I measure my life against a reliable standard. Increasingly, I find meaning there. (Ehrlich 1997, xii–xiii)

Ehrlich knows that the lifestyle she has chosen for her children is different from her own and also from her previous enjoyment of shellfish, pork dishes, and cheeseburgers, all foods she has given up in order to embark upon this new culinary adventure. By keeping kosher, Elizabeth, Jacob, and their children forge an embodied connection to the experience of their relatives, both living and dead, who organized their lives according to similar principles and took part in the very same rituals of their Jewish faith in Canada, Poland, Spain, and Israel. After deciding to raise her children to be fully initiated into the Jewish faith, Ehrlich wonders whether she is alienating them from their American national culture, rearing them to be separatists, and maybe move away to settle in Israel.

Ehrlich grew up in a secular household, where Jewishness was merely a marker of ethnicity, rather than a source of diasporic connections to other communities around the world. For Ehrlich's father in Detroit, Israel symbolized an escape route, a possible place to run to if things ever got to be too bad.[2] Ehrlich's saga of return to Jewish customs and traditions is only made possible by how far her own parents had strayed from their observant progenitors. The Detroit of Ehrlich's youth was a cosmopolitan enough city for two diasporic communities like African Americans and Jews to overlap and come into contact during the decades of Black Power and civil rights. However, after her decision to keep kosher and live a Jewish life, Ehrlich felt her new choices would cost her the friendship of those who were not equally invested in their own heritage, who might reasonably assume her family's embrace of gastronomic conservatism meant they had become judgmental or even intolerant of difference.

Ehrlich's discussion of her culinary conversion acknowledges her choice to keep a kosher kitchen was an artificial, though not a meaningless, gesture because she is a nonbeliever. Faced with their son's request to pick up some KFC on the way home, Ehrlich pondered the different sense of obligation or emotional debt their shared nutritional regimen occasioned in each spouse: "Here is the difference between those returning to tradition (me) and those securely rooted but not absolutist in life. My husband could have taken the kids and said to the teenager behind the counter, '"Chicken, please, and fries, and Coke—no bacon or butter or ice cream.' Good enough, *shoyn*, already" (Ehrlich 1997, 260). Jacob's traditional upbringing ingrained in him such a strong sense of identification with his religious dietary regimen that he could be flexible in accommodating his children's spontaneous requests for fast food. As someone brand new to *kashrut*, who had not yet fully stocked her kitchen with all of the different sets of dishes, cooking utensils, and sponges for meat, dairy, and neutral meals, Ehrlich saw the fast food as a potential threat to her commitment to this nutritional identity:

> But it was unkosher chicken, not fed or killed or examined according to Jewish law, and then it was maybe dipped in milk and fried in I don't know what, and served with macaroni and cheese and a roll with butter and string beans with bacon bits and a complimentary ice cream for dessert. Solid food, not to be scorned, but not what I wanted to allow, just then, even just this once. (Ehrlich 1997, 260)

---

2. This was her family's view. Jewish identity is no longer considered to refer to one particular ethnic group; people of all racial, national, or ethnic backgrounds can convert to Judaism or be descended from people who practiced the faith and identified as Jewish.

Ehrlich's acknowledgement that nonkosher food is "not to be scorned" demonstrates her continuing struggle to align her ideological embrace of diversity as a desirable social goal, and the exclusionary outlook at the heart of the rabbinical pronouncements that define *kashrut*. This episode appears in italics on its own, as an interlude of sorts between two formal chapters. As such, it does not have an accompanying recipe, but, as if to soften the pain of transitioning to a new way of eating, it is sandwiched between recipes for two sweets: "Irene's *Pareve* Kugel" (Ehrlich 1997, 244) and "Granny's Cheese Danishes" (Ehrlich 1997, 270). She did not come to her conviction to embrace the performative aspects of Judaism lightly; *Miriam's Kitchen* chronicles Ehrlich's slow process toward keeping kosher and her mixed feelings about how adopting this tradition into the day-to-day life of the family distanced her from her non-Jewish friends and nonkosher relatives.

In a similar vein to Ehrlich's wish to honor her mother-in-law's suffering by adhering to the Jewish dietary laws she held sacred, acclaimed novelist Jonathan Safran Foer confesses that one motivation behind his conscious return to the Passover tradition that has sustained the Jewish people through a diaspora lasting millennia was his desire to make his immigrant grandparents proud of him.[3] Another, equally important factor was becoming a father. Foer, who edited the *New American Haggadah*, sets himself up as the spokesperson for the new class of secular American Jews who have chosen to reclaim their diasporic cultural heritage as a way of signaling their entry into adult life and also a way to honor their relatives:

> Our grandparents were immigrants to America, but natives to Judaism. We are the opposite: fluent in "American Idol," but unschooled in Jewish heroes. And so we act like immigrants around Judaism: cautious, rejecting, self-conscious, and feigning (or achieving) indifference. In the foreign country of our faith, our need for a good guidebook is urgent. (2012a, n.p.)

By applying the metaphor of the "immigrant" to describe his generation's distant relationship to the faith of their ancestors, Foer suggests that membership within an imagined community—whether formed on the basis of a shared religious, national, or diasporic self-identification—depends upon constant performance of one's status as an insider. My own reading of the

---

3. In his work of literary journalism, *Eating Animals* (2009), Foer discusses his grandmother's refusal to break *kashrut* by eating pork offered to her when she faced near-starvation in the forests in Europe because then she would have absolutely compromised the beliefs that had made her life worth living.

ambivalence immigrants feel toward the idea of assimilation and nativism is somewhat at odds with Foer's simple calculus here, but his articulation serves to illustrate the contrast between the different generations' relationship to Judaism.

A haggadah is a written text retelling the story of the exodus of the Israelites from bondage in Egypt that is read during the Seder meal on the eve of Passover. The meal itself consists of four glasses of wine consumed at specific points in the story, accompanied by appetizers, a main course, and dessert. As a cultural object, the haggadah itself is a part of an invented tradition. Rabbinic scholars are in agreement that the Passover ritual changed after the destruction of the Temple. According to Joshua Kulp, "current scholars agree that many of the Seder customs as described in rabbinic literatures were innovations of the post-70 FH period, and nearly all scholars agree that there was no Seder or haggadah while the temple still stood" (Kulp 2005, 110). Thus, adopting and adapting the haggadah to suit the needs of a dispersed people is itself in keeping with both the cultural and religious traditions of Judaism.

Echoing Ehrlich, Foer explains that he created a *New American Haggadah* to inspire others like him to reclaim the Seder as a meaningful Jewish tradition. Rather than being the product of any spiritual awakening, Foer was motivated to pass these rich cultural traditions as his patrimony to his children. The *New American Haggadah* he edited serves a dual purpose, depending on how it is put to use: religious Jews can turn to it as a vernacular guide to the proper observance of the ritual meal, while secular Jews and others who wish to partake of the occasion can marvel at the beauty of language that consciously heightens the dramatic elements of the original story of Exodus.[4] In interviews to promote the new book, Foer spoke of his desire to connect in a more meaningful way to his Jewish heritage, something he had taken for granted as his birthright without really learning about it until he became a father. At that point, he realized that the old standby of many an American Jewish household, the *Maxwell House Haggadah* handed out as promotional literature during Passover, would no longer do as a guide now that he expected more out of this celebration. That corporate Haggadah, though serviceable, failed to engage his higher faculties; it did not appeal to him aesthetically or intellectually. As a secular, non-Hebrew-speaking American Jew, Foer felt the need to have a text that resonated with him and

---

4. Kulp also points out that religious Christians have begun celebrating Passover in small but increasing numbers.

his family in a transcendent language suitable for the occasion, so he set out to create his own, and he secured the cooperation of fellow novelist, Nathan Englander, as translator, as well as four other writers to serve as commentators in the work: Lemony Snicket, Nathaniel Deutsch, Jeffrey Goldberg, and Rebecca Newberger Goldstein.[5] As a cultural intervention for newly invested Jewish diasporics living in the United States, this book is an example of exactly the kind of activation of identities "not continuous with those of the nation-state" that Joseph contends is now in vogue.

Affirming African Diasporic Connections

Novelist and playwright Ntozake Shange's celebratory appropriation of the myriad foodways of the transnational African diaspora reflects the nonhierarchical, multicultural, and Afrocentric outlook she has adopted and according to which she hopes to bring up her child. Although she mentions her mother, Ellie, she is far from the only or even the primary source of culinary information shaping Shange's outlook on the cultural vibrancy of African diaspora foodways she seeks to recover. She credits both cultural capital—like her travels, reading of literature, listening to jazz, appreciating artwork, and dancing—as well as her personal relationships with family and friends with exposing her to dishes eaten at many different outposts of the African diaspora, which she then incorporated into her own cooking repertoire and shared with her readers in *If I Can Cook / You Know God Can*. Throughout this fluid and evocative memoir, Shange invokes the notion of invented traditions as constitutive parts of the African diaspora experience, such as the rise of Juneteenth celebrations, which she ascribes to communal belatedness: "since they'd missed the end of slavery by two years, black Texans created their own Independence Day, Juneteenth, which is still celebrated wherever black Texans and their descendants or admirers dwell" (Shange 1998, 60). Merely by discussing this holiday, including an appropriate Texas barbeque recipe to celebrate it, and mentioning in the same chapter that she had become adept at rodeo barrel racing in Texas, Shange proclaims her membership in a Texas branch of an African-diasporic community. As we saw in chapter 3, regional identities are important in all of these texts, so they are not to be forgotten within the diaspora.

---

5. While some of these writers are famous for their humor and satire, this work is not in any way a parody, nor is it an oversimplification of a complex ritual. In fact, it is more contextual than the *Maxwell House Haggadah* and amplifies the ritual through the inclusion of commentary from multiple vantage points.

Shange pursues an activist diasporic practice and outlook throughout *If I Can Cook / You Know God Can* that builds upon conversations among and between different groups of Afro-descended peoples to better understand one another's history. She highlights the degree to which these diasporas have truly interconnected when she observes: "Black nationalists, black Jews, and black Muslims have a profound effect on the daily lives of all classes of mainland African-Americans as well as those of us spread throughout the hemisphere" (Shange 1998, 88). Her musings take her in unexpected directions; rather than share a recipe for a Jewish or Muslim dish in this chapter, Shange includes a vegetarian dish featuring seitan, or "wheatmeat," in honor of yet another diasporic group, the Rastafarians from Jamaica, whose religion promotes a plant-based diet. The dish is for "Company's Comin' Wheatmeat with Organic Brown Rice/Good Salad" (Shange 1998, 89–91). Shange's attempts at solidarity with vegetarians and what she calls "Negroized" or Afrocentric meat-free dishes ended when she discovered that such healthy food interfered with the hectic tempo of urban life.

When Shange decided to introduce her daughter, Savannah, to the cherished family traditions of her youth despite being alone for the Christmas holiday, she took the toddler shopping around the city for the ingredients to make a traditional Southern New Year's eve meal:

> I was determined that Savannah, my child, should have a typical Owens/ Williams holiday, even though I was not a gaggle of aunts and uncles, cousins, second and third cousins twice removed, or even relatives from Oklahoma or Carolina. I was just me, Mommy, in one body and with many memories of not enough room for all the toddlers at the tables. How could I re-create the smells of okra and rice, Hoppin' John, baked ham, pig's feet, chitlins, collard greens and cornbread with syrup if I was goin'ta [sic] feed two people? (Shange 1998, 7)

Finding appropriate substitutes adds an intentionality that enhances the satisfaction people feel when performing the ritual. All texts discussed in this chapter share this valorization of "mindfulness." Shange's celebration is "invented" in Hobsbawm's sense not because it is not an accurate representation of her family's New Year's spread, but because it is replicated only in terms of the food items served, rather than held in the communal spirit of the event that brings the generations together under one roof. Her embodied memory of "not enough room for all the toddlers at the table" is starkly at odds with the setup for her and her daughter's meal, where there is ample room and no other children present. Shange resurrects this tradition years later not by restaging the actual meal, but by sharing with her readers the recipes she followed that night. Thus, the chapter includes recipes written much like the receipts of nineteenth- and early-twentieth-century cookbooks, each condensed down into a single paragraph, rather than making use of white space for aesthetic principles and taking up an entire page. The featured dishes are "Pig's Tails by Instinct" and "Hoppin John (Black-eyed Peas and Rice)," "Collard Greens to Bring You Money," and "French-fried Chitlins" (Shange 1998, 9–11). In her prefatory remarks to this last recipe, Shange shares a little of her status as the grandchild of immigrants: "My father, whose people were Canadian and did not eat chitlins at all, told me my daughter's French-fried Chitlin taste like lobster" (Shange 1998, 11), thereby further complicating her earlier claim of the canonical status of the New Year's meal.

Although Shange spends so much time discussing the Afro-diasporic community she feels herself a part of, the Afrocentric holiday of Kwanzaa is noticeably absent from this memoir. What makes this absence especially ironic is that Shange had previously included a Kwanzaa recipe as a plot point in her first novel, *Sassafrass, Cypress and Indigo* (1982); it appears within a letter the mother sends her oldest daughter, who has decided to celebrate Kwanzaa instead of Christmas, "Mama's Kwanza [*sic*] Recipe (for Sassafrass): Duck with Oyster Stuffing" (Shange 1996, 132). That "fictional" recipe is formatted like conventional ones, with the ingredients listed first and the steps for preparation listed in their own separate paragraph. This recipe symbolizes the effort the matriarch character makes to continue being a part of her daughter's life, even when that young woman has chosen to embrace radically different traditions from those of her childhood. It also reflects the ambivalence Kwanzaa continues to engender within various African American communities. Because its origins are tied to a particular historical moment and radical set of politics, it is not a tradition that has become universally embraced.

The Afrocentric holiday of Kwanzaa is the brainchild of Dr. Maulana Karenga, a controversial figure in the Black Nationalist movement who served jail time, and later became a professor of Africana studies. Developed in 1966, Kwanzaa was the result of a social experiment aimed at counteracting the negative emotional impact of enduring sustained racism, individual and institutional, through a syncretic holiday tradition that brings together multiple African harvest-festival customs and foodstuffs, given coherence through the use of the trade-language of Swahili. Like Hanukah, which is observed over eight nights, the Kwanzaa celebration also spans multiple days. Each one affirms one of the seven core principles, or *nguzo saba:* unity (*umoja*), self-determination (*kujichagulia*), collective work and responsibility (*ujima*), cooperative economics (*ujamma*), purpose (*nia*), creativity (*kuumba*), and faith (*Imani*).

As a reporter for *The New York Times* and sometime food blogger, Copage first learned about Kwanzaa during a visit to the American Museum of Natural History but only adopted this cultural tradition into his family a few years later, after the birth of his son, Evan. Wanting to instill a sense of pride in their African American heritage in his son, Copage considered making up a ritual of his own, but decided against it. He embraces Kwanzaa for the diasporic opportunities it offers for "metaphysical bonding with other African Americans" (Copage 1991, xiv). Copage's reasons for incorporating this new holiday tradition into his family life resemble Foer's in their impetus (fatherhood) and diasporic scope as well as in the tradition's value as an emotional commodity. The culinary delights of such a holiday are not lost on Copage, especially since he frames *Kwanzaa* as a primer in the form of a cookbook featuring assorted recipes from Afro-diasporic or pan-African cultures:

> I thought about my goals for Evan and decided that Kwanzaa was the best lens through which to view the landscape of the African diaspora and the lessons it has to teach. Because it is only one week long, and because of the ceremony, and because it climaxes with a glorious feast, Kwanzaa has an intensity and focus that provides the perfect atmosphere for my son to experience the joys of being black. (Copage 1991, xv)

Once again, intentionality and mindfulness lend an invented tradition its special celebratory power for the family who chooses to observe it. To reflect the diasporic scope of the holiday and its adaptable traditions, Copage's *Kwanzaa* decenters narrative authority by including multiple anecdotes from various families who celebrate the holiday and contribute their own recipes to the volume. In a similar way, Foer's *The New American Haggadah* also pursues this diasporic decentralization by including ongoing commentaries by four distinct "experts" listed under the headings "library," "nation," "house of study," and "playground," the last of which is meant to keep children's attention. Whereas any Haggadah follows the proscribed order of the Seder meal itself, which marks the start of Passover and involves the ritual retelling of the Exodus story, Kwanzaa highlights various different strategies for customizing the structure of the holiday observance according to one's particular family situations. This openness to customization is part of the appeal—the tradition is flexible enough to accommodate family preference and busy schedules, thereby making Kwanzaa more similar to Festivus (which has no set date) than to the Seder.

Copage explains how his family takes advantage of this flexibility: "There is a wide spectrum of ways to observe Kwanzaa. My family, like many others, takes an a la carte approach. We decided we'd have one Kwanzaa meal in the middle of the weeklong holiday" (Copage 1991, xxii). Feasts are seen as a key component to the celebration but also as a potential distraction away from other rituals associated with each night of Kwanzaa, so Copage reminds his readers that "planning the ceremony should be the very first thing you do" (Copage 1991, xxvi). While food preparation provides a link back to a long and troubled history of African influences in the New World, such as the ancestors' stoic endurance of slavery and adaptation and survival in times of adversity and discrimination, the improvised rituals connect African-descended individuals to their successful contemporaries and to future generations as they create new, positive narratives of their contributions to the advancement of a vibrant and interconnected diasporic community. The book contains over one hundred family recipes to choose from in preparing the celebration. Not included among these, but described receipt-like in the introduction, is the meal Copage and his family ate the first time they celebrated Kwanzaa:

> Our fist meal consisted of dishes that brought forth sweet memories of my childhood. I remembered helping my grandmother make collard greens, especially the arduous task of washing dirt from the leaves (and getting bawled out if someone got a gritty mouthful during dinner), and I remembered sorting and discarding the bad black-eyed peas for the Hoppin John she cooked. I remembered visiting West Africa when I was eighteen and tasting the spicy tingle of peanut soup for the first time. And of course there was a lifetime of cornbread. (Copage 1991, xxii)

Copage's effort to feed his family a memorable meal from his childhood recalls Shange's attempt to recreate the New Year's celebrations of her toddlerhood. Neither event had religious overtones; both featured traditional foods from the South as a commemoration of how their African-descended ancestors forged ties of family and community by cooking and eating together. Like Shange does with the Rastafarian recipe for "wheatmeat," Copage suggests customizing the feast to support vegetarian lifestyles or serving dishes from a particular region, like the Caribbean.

Postmodern Reclamations of Invented Family Traditions

Like Kwanzaa, Festivus is an artificially created celebration that grew out of one family's discontent with the prevalence of consumer culture. Unlike the Afrocentric holiday, however, its origins were more modest: the faux holiday of Festivus was meant to remain a family tradition. However, in the most self-conscious example of gastrographical revisionism discussed in this chapter, Dan O'Keefe not only incorporated his family tradition into the plotline of *Seinfeld*, the television sitcom for which he was a writer, but fully seven years after the show's finale, he went on to publish a memoir detailing the origins of the tradition within his Irish American family, *The Real Festivus: The True Story Behind America's Favorite Made-Up Holiday*.

Primarily because of its artificial or invented origins, the *Seinfeld* version of "Festivus" has now transcended its roots and become a constitutive part of global popular culture celebrated by hard-core fans of the show, whether they are Irish like the O'Keefes, Jewish like a lot of the show's cast members, Italian-ish like the Costanza family, or just plain crazy about the sitcom. Despite the celebration's anticonsumerist roots, a cottage industry has sprung up around the sale of Festivus cards and aluminum Festivus poles. The food industry has also jumped into the bandwagon—Ben & Jerry's came out with a limited-edition Festivus flavor (brown sugar ice cream with gingerbread cookies and ginger caramel swirls), while *Salon.com*, *Epicurious*, and *HuffPost Food* have all published recipes for appropriate meals and libations to celebrate the occasion. The spread of this tradition beyond the television screen may, at first, seem like a sign that generations of people feel so disconnected from their individual heritage that they actually model their lived experience on televised simulacra of imagined communities. However, I contend that it is precisely this identification with urban life that continues to appeal to fans who themselves may live far from the families and traditions with which they grew up.

As a manual and guide to the titular holiday, O'Keefe's *The Real Festivus* is set up very much like Foer's *New American Haggadah* and Copage's *Kwanzaa*. Instead of narrating the flight out of Egypt or proclaiming the wisdom of the seven Afrocentric guiding principles, *The Real Festivus* chronicles the inception of the holiday, tracing its roots back to 1966 when the family patriarch devised it during a date with the woman who would become his wife. This was the same year in which the first Kwanzaa was celebrated by its creator. Where the haggadah begins the celebration of the Seder with the question, "What makes this night different from all other nights?" (Foer 2012a, 21), O'Keefe opens his memoir with the following interrogative: "Festivus: What's Up with That?" (O'Keefe 2005, iii). From there, the book includes chapters discussing appropriate "Symbols and Decorations," "The Poem of Festivus," "The Music of Festivus," and especially "Festivus Dinner and Gifts," featuring three recipes by O'Keefe's mother: "No-Cream Cream of Chicken Soup" (O'Keefe 2005, 43), "Beef Stew from Galena, Illinois" (O'Keefe 2005, 44–45), and "'Three of a Kind' Ice Cream" (O'Keefe 2005, 46). Finally, the meal is consumed by candlelight, as are the Kwanzaa and Seder feasts. Nothing about this family version of the holiday is tied in any way to their Irish roots or Catholic faith.

What is so oddly touching about a book whose primary purpose is to profit off of the popularity of the Festivus episode of *Seinfeld*, is how seriously it takes the charge of reclaiming this tradition for the O'Keefe family. This is a son's book about his belated and renewed appreciation for a quirky family tradition that has now been altered and appropriated by the masses: "We may not have thought so at the time, but we were lucky to have Festivus. It was a celebration of family and an exorcism of the demons that menaced it" (O'Keefe 2005, 134). The redeeming virtue he finds in it was its affirmation of the value of family and the bonds it creates. Though he now looks upon Festivus as his patrimony, the younger O'Keefe does not share his father's anticonsumerism; in fact, not only has the popularity of the sitcom version made him more famous than anything else he has written, but it has also earned him money, something he is eager to exploit when he exhorts readers on the last page to "buy other copies of this book for your friends. It makes a lovely gift." Cashing in on a family brand is not the worst outcome of inventing a new tradition.

Another writer who resorts to parody as she both mines and reclaims the peculiar celebrations that characterized her youth is Anya Von Bremzen. This James-Beard-award-winning food writer sets out to mock the invented traditions the Soviet Union promoted by "re-creating" dishes that are the touchstones of her family's experience living under the various Communist regimes in her recent memoir with recipes, *Mastering the Art of Soviet Cooking*. Von Bremzen has mined this gastronomic patrimony before, in her first cookbook, *Please to the Table: The Russian Cookbook* (1990), cowritten with John Welchman, a panoramic compendium of recipes from all parts of the Soviet Union despite both its subtitle and the social upheaval that caused the demise of the Iron Curtain after the fall of the Berlin Wall in 1989. Writing well after most of the former Soviet Republics have reclaimed their independence, and with the wisdom of hindsight, Von Bremzen revisits the joint trauma of her Soviet childhood and her dramatic immigration to the United States. Together with her mother, Larissa, Von Bremzen engages in a strategic performance of re-creating the simulacra of Soviet food as it was discussed or celebrated throughout her childhood either by propagandist news releases about abundant crops that never saw their way to the local markets, or else by detailed reports of the elaborate feasts the Soviet leaders hosted to impress foreign dignitaries with their country's supposed prosperity.

Though the ironic banquets and culinary "reenactments" of meals emblematic of distinct periods in Russian history, from the "extravagant czarist-era dinner" (Von Bremzen 2013, 8) that opens the memoir's first chapter to retro-Soviet meals like the "herring under fur coat" (Von Bremzen 2013, 287) or upscale, gourmet versions of former "communal-apartment dishes" that have become characteristic of Putin's time in power amuse the mother-daughter immigrant couple, they also serve a more important role. As much as observing Kwanzaa or gathering with friends and family to celebrate the Seder help members of the Jewish and African diasporic communities admit the trauma of life in bondage, and transcend it through the memory work performed by those rituals, so does this elaborate charade help Von Bremzen and her mother publicly discuss, and hopefully exorcise, their shared "memories of wartime rationing cards and grotesque shared kitchens in communal apartments" (Von Bremzen 2013, 5). Von Bremzen resorts to a culinary allusion to express her reasons for engaging in Palmié-style "gastrographical revisionism" when she calls her taste memories of Soviet food "poisoned madeleines" in the prologue of *Mastering the Art of Soviet Cooking*. Her reference to Proust and the memory-enabling cookie that triggered the narrator's *Remembrance of Things Past* stems from her mother's habit of reading the French novelist's works out loud to young Anya to help them both pass the time at home. In this acknowledgement of the lingering legacy of trauma, Von Bremzen's text is aligned with the African American memories of slavery in Copage's *Kwanzaa* and Shange's *If I Can Cook / You Know God Can*, as well as the references to the Holocaust in *Miriam's Kitchen* and the Jewish experiences of slavery in Egypt memorialized in *The New American Haggadah*.

Rather than invent a whole new tradition to mark the family's transition from their Soviet subsistence to an American life, Anya's mother Larissa proposes that they engage in a limited, one-year experiment of "eating and cooking our way through decade after decade of Soviet life, using her kitchen and dining room as a time machine and an incubator of memories" (Von Bremzen 2013, 5). Two iconic recipes stand out from the rest for the way in which they require communal collaboration to put them together.

The first is for "Salat Olivier," a mayonnaise-laden staple of communal kitchens. The original version of the salad dates back to mid-nineteenth-century Moscow, where French chef Lucien Olivier of L'Hermitage concocted an elaborate composed salad that Von Bremzen claims the locals later appropriated. The homemade version of this dish was generally prepared to accompany state-sponsored celebrations, and residents of communal apartments pooled together their assorted resources to arrive at the ten ingredients necessary for its preparation: root vegetables (potatoes, carrots), fruit (apples, cucumbers), peas, pickles, proteins (eggs and chicken when available), and assorted greens (scallions and dill). Von Bremzen's prefatory remarks to the recipe describe it as an indelible part of the Russian diaspora: "Variations of the salad traveled the world with White Russian émigrés. To this day, I'm amazed to encounter it under its generic name, 'Russian salad,' at steakhouses in Buenos Aires, railway stations in Istanbul, or as part of Korean or Spanish or Iranian appetizer spreads. Amazed and just a little bit proud" (Von Bremzen 2013, 316). This act of looking for, and finding, the salad on the menus of the places where she goes to eat as a professional food writer is Von Bremzen's way of performing her membership in the imagined community of the Soviet/Russian diaspora. Her mother, Larissa, takes a different approach, reclaiming and updating the salad for her own purposes by using fresh vegetables and substituting crab meat for the chicken that was usually available in the Soviet apartments. In this way, she strikes out at the scarcity that marked her life under Communist rule by incorporating just a bit more luxury into what has come to be the equivalent of a national dish. This recasting of an artificial tradition to serve one's own ends recalls Daniel O'Keefe's decision to monetize his version of the Festivus holiday.

The second dish that punctuates Von Bremzen's experience of Soviet life as a child is borscht. She describes two primary versions, the thin, vegetarian broth her mother made while raising her as a single parent, and the luscious concoction that her father makes to impress his ex-wife and daughter upon their return to the motherland. Of the former, Von Bremzen says: "To my childhood palate, *borshch* (as Russians spell borscht) was less a soup than a kind of Soviet quotidian destiny: something to be endured along with Moscow tap water and the endless grayness of socialist winter" (Von Bremzen 2013, 318). This is a symbol of their poverty and her mother's resourcefulness in being able to cobble something together that would feed the two of them on what little she earned. The second kind, however, is revelatory for Von Bremzen: "the mythical 'real' Ukrainian borsch we knew from descriptions in State-approved recipe booklets authored by hack 'gastronomic historians'" (Von Bremzen 2013, 318). Though Von Bremzen grew up to be a legitimate rather than a "hack" gastronomic historian, she was nonetheless surprised to find that her father's version of this dish is not only every bit as appealing as the propaganda promised borscht could be, but even better, through his unexpectedly artistic touches, like juicing beets to enhance the finished stew's rich color. By including the recipe for her father's ersatz version of borscht, with its addition of beans and mushrooms, in her memoir with recipes and proudly declaring it to be much better than the "real thing" she has tasted in Ukraine, Von Bremzen reestablishes a family connection that helps her feel rooted to her Soviet life, even as the Soviet Union is no more. Like O'Keefe, Von Bremzen has chosen to profit, both personally and financially, from her father's ingenuity.

This meditation upon the artificial nature of invented traditions is a fitting way to end a book that takes as its topic a highly artificial way of being in the world—that of permanently uprooting oneself from a given national and cultural background only to start again elsewhere through the legal process of immigration. For the immigrant, most every part of everyday life has to be refashioned anew, whether through a stubborn preservation of the "old ways," a wholesale embrace of the new, or some combination of both. Starting a family or just the mere desire to pass on what one has learned to the next generation serves as an impetus to share one's culture and tradition, and what better way than to do so in celebration around a table brimming with delicious food?

Conclusion

Talking Turkey
The Thanksgiving Holiday as the Measure of Assimilation

I would like to close this study with a brief consideration of Thanksgiving, arguably the holiday that most clearly invokes the common myth of the United States as a nation made up of immigrants, starting with the starving Pilgrims who depended upon the bounty and advice of the local Natives for their ability to adapt their agricultural techniques to the local climate. Since there is no surfeit of Thanksgiving-themed memoirs, I will instead turn to a brief discussion of three Hollywood films that directly depict Thanksgiving celebrations as occasions in which immigrants to the United States can publicly perform their full membership within the national imaginary: *Avalon* (1990), *Pieces of April* (2003), and *What's Cooking?* (2000). Representing various cinematic genres and aimed at different audiences, all three films prominently feature immigrants observing the Thanksgiving feast. I put my readings of these films in conversation with Roger Ebert's reviews of each, since this Pulitzer Prize–winning film critic wrote about being the grandson of German immigrants and, thus, was especially alert to these texts' treatment of the immigrant experience. Finally, I pause to consider a few recent newspaper human-interest stories discussing how immigrants feel about taking part in the Thanksgiving holiday celebrations, paying particular attention to whether the human-interest stories emphasize the featured immigrants' discussion of food as representing strategies of cultural assimilation (serving turkey, mashed potatoes, and cranberry sauce) or culinary domestication (using the seasonings associated with the cuisine of their birthplaces to make the bland bird more palatable). Since this is a self-selected group of immigrants who agree to share their stories with a national audience, I end this study by comparing their views of themselves and their foodways to the narrative strategies deployed by the memoirs with recipes discussed in the previous chapters.

These three Hollywood films released at the end of the twentieth and beginning of the twenty-first century illustrate how immigrants are depicted in contemporary iconography surrounding Thanksgiving celebrations: *Avalon* is a nostalgic look at Jewish immigration to Baltimore during the first half of the twentieth century; *What's Cooking?* depicts interconnected neighborhood celebrations in multicultural Los Angeles; and *Pieces of April* portrays a building-wide Thanksgiving celebration in a run-down New York City neighborhood. Read in that order, the films demonstrate the immigrant experience in the United States as a domestic, but somewhat insular, exercise in patriotism, growing increasingly more interconnected through time and happenstance. None of the films question the iconic role of the turkey, that quintessentially American fowl, in the meal, a significant element since each film deals with recently arrived immigrants and their families rather than only with second- or third-generation ethnic Americans. In the discussions that follow, I will examine each film's treatment of the holiday meal and its immigrant characters as emblematic of its overall view of the myth of America as a nation of immigrants through their respective deployment of two tropes: the "myth of return," and "culinary policing." The myth of return has to do with the notion that families of all faiths gathered together for Thanksgiving as a communal secular celebration, whereas not everyone observed the same religious holidays the rest of the year.[1] Culinary policing is distinct from the concept of "gastronomic surveillance" discussed earlier, because the emphasis is not so much on enforcing the uniformity in eating, since Thanksgiving involves a feast served family-style, but rather on the adherence to culinary rules (of etiquette or of cooking procedures) that have emotional significance rather than prove one's assimilation to a national norm.

---

1. My use of "myth of return" is an adaptation of Elizabeth Pleck's discussion of "the ritual of returning home at Thanksgiving" in the nineteenth century. As she defines it, "A man could be self-made and an obedient son, so long as he reunited with his family for Thanksgiving" (1999, 775).

Immigrant Thanksgiving Celebrations on Film

Barry Levinson's *Avalon* earned him an Academy Award nomination as a screenwriter. The movie follows a Russian Jewish immigrant family that struggles to maintain its traditions as an extended family. In his positive review of *Avalon*, film critic Roger Ebert points to the movie's most quotable scene, which, coincidentally, takes place during a Thanksgiving dinner at one of the brothers' homes in the suburbs. Gabriel, the most old-fashioned of the brothers, who disapproves of this move away from the city and continually arrives late to family celebrations, is distraught when he walks in as usual on Thanksgiving Day, only to find that the family has begun eating a while earlier. He utters the astonished interrogative that has become synonymous with the movie: "You cut the turkey without me?" Whereas Ebert pauses on the climax as the pivotal aspect of the scene that marks the subsequent breakdown of the extended family structure, I choose to focus on how food and appetite are figured within the scene as it unfolds as evidence of the Krichinskys' desire to assimilate to mainstream society. The family matriarch remarks that Thanksgiving is a "funny" holiday that "makes no sense" precisely because it requires the consumption of a protein, turkey, which they do not consume at any other time of year. This is an acknowledgement that in eating the iconic foods of the season—roast turkey, mashed potatoes, cranberry sauce—the family is performing a different national and/or ethnic identity than the one that most accurately represents their particular tastes and culinary sensibilities. The only visible concession to the children's tastes is the conspicuous presence of glass containers of soft drinks, two of which appear to be colas and a third one that is orange soda.

The family's grandchildren, or third generation, are key to this move toward an American identity. Their hunger and impatience, voiced from their separate kids' table, are what finally sway the patriarch to give in to the half-immigrants', or second generation's, persuasive argument in favor of breaking with tradition and starting the meal without the latecomer. Then, the shot cuts to the house's front walk, where Gabriel and his wife are seen approaching the door. Time has passed, and by the time Gabriel enters the dining area, we have heard a youngster complain about his mashed potatoes touching his turkey, declaring that he hates it when food touches. This minor tantrum prepares the audience for the seemingly childish outburst that follows, when Gabriel realizes that the family has begun eating without him and summarily leaves with his wife to return to the city. He takes the family's break with tradition as a personal insult and will not listen to his younger brother's pleas to stay. The brother, however, appeals to the children's appetites as the reason to not "stand on ceremony with the family," saying, "The young ones are hungry. They carry on. They make a commotion." This shift in emphasis from the family elders as the head of the family to the youngest generations as the ones whose needs must be met and who should not be kept hungry marks the real aspect of the family's assimilation into an American, rather than a European, dining context. American families do not regard meals with the same level of formality as do the Europeans, and thus, would prefer to pacify the annoying children than to make them behave in deference to their elders. This is what marks both the parents (U.S.-born children) and their offspring (the third generation of the family) as Americans, whereas the grandparents' generation remains indelibly marked by the experience of immigration, which makes them wary of giving up their cultural capital.

The prodigal aspect of the Thanksgiving cultural narrative is the organizing principle the other two movies under discussion use to usher in their investigations of how many different kinds of Americans—those from the establishment, minority backgrounds, and recent arrivals—intersect as they strive to contribute to a vibrant and diverse nation. Unsurprisingly, both *What's Cooking?* and *Pieces of April* take place in big cities—Los Angeles and New York, respectively—instead of the suburbs where the controversial Thanksgiving feast takes place in *Avalon*. The high concentration of people from different backgrounds and ages makes urban areas ideal for exploring this type of action, whereas the relative anonymity of the suburbs, symbolized through the mushrooming developments of houses that all look alike, reinforces the tendency toward family insularity.

Although families are at the very heart of both *What's Cooking?* and *Pieces of April*, children are not necessarily central to the depiction of family strife. Instead, extramarital affairs, divorce, same-sex relationships, and interracial romances are all plot points that complicate a family's ability to enjoy this domestic holiday in peace. *What's Cooking?* features interlocking stories about four families that live in the same neighborhood but do not really socialize with one another: one is Latino, another Jewish, a third African American, and a fourth is Vietnamese American. Through the "myth of return" motif, external differences in their family makeup are less obvious than they would be otherwise: only the Vietnamese family has three generations living in the same household on a regular basis, whereas relatives make their way to the family home from college or other states in order to properly celebrate the holiday "with family" in the other households. The multicultural nature of this huge cast of characters is in keeping with the overall demographics of Los Angeles, and the presence of both the

Vietnamese and Latino families are reminders of the city's proximity both to Mexico, by land, and to Asia, via air. The relatively warm weather and sunny glow framing each family as they busily prepare for the feast firmly establishes the film as a West Coast, rather than a national, product.

The aspect of this film that warrants most critical attention in this context is the depiction of "culinary policing" that takes place within almost every household. The self-appointed expert in each instance argues for a specific set of culinary practices that are inherently linked with a traditional performance of ethnic or national identity. Roger Ebert comments upon two such instances in his review of the film, and I cite him here to serve as a counterpoint to the two other examples I will supply. His first observation has to do with the teenage daughter of the Vietnamese family:

> They all serve turkey in one way or another, surrounded by traditional dishes from their nationalities; some are tired of turkey and try to disguise it, while an Americanized Vietnamese girl sees the chili paste going on and complains, "Why do you want to make the turkey taste like everything else we eat?" (Ebert 2000)

The girl's complaint about her grandmother's attempt to make the turkey appetizing to the family's Vietnamese palate is precisely the opposite of the sentiment the Krichinsky family matriarch uttered about the inherent funniness of turkey as an outlier in the family's culinary repertoire. Although the Jewish Krichinskys want to assimilate to mainstream society, they resent having to "eat American" food in order to become Americans, whereas the Nguyen children already are American and thus resent having to perform their Vietnamese identity at home to placate the anxieties of their parents and grandmother. The mother comes up with a pragmatic solution: only half of the turkey will be seasoned with the chili paste, while the other is not, thus taking both generations' culinary preferences into consideration. While this is a promising way to resolve conflict, the turkey actually burns in the oven, since the family becomes distraught upon finding out their oldest son is not coming home from college to join them. The audience never gets to see the family members have to choose, then, between each of the "traditional" preparations for the turkey: traditional American or traditionally Vietnamese. Instead, fast food comes to the rescue, and the family ends up happily eating Kentucky Fried Chicken together.

A similar set of tensions takes place in the African American household, where the mother-in-law disapproves of the daughter-in-law's decision to forego the traditional macaroni and cheese, which Ebert describes as "an obligatory item at every African-American feast" in his review; so, she goes ahead and makes it herself, over the daughter-in-law's objections. When the wife proudly serves the golden, roasted turkey to the assembled family and friends, it falls straight through the middle of the table, thus symbolizing the fragile state of family relationships. The marriage is on the rocks because the father has been having an affair; the oldest son's attempt to connect with his African American roots leads him to participate in petty vandalism against his father's boss, a Republican politician; and the mother-in-law holds the wife responsible for her son's inattention to her. The threat of assimilation here is not to American culture per se, but rather what worries the mother-in-law is the looming prospect of her son and his family becoming so bourgeois that they lose touch with the more working-class African American community to which she belongs.

All four of the featured families live in a racially integrated neighborhood, rather than in ethnic enclaves. While some degree of meddling, or culinary policing, takes place in the other two families, the Jewish and the Latino ones, they manage to get through the cooking process of the turkey without any large incidents. The Latino family's daughter's Asian American boyfriend, who is actually the son of the Vietnamese family, decides to endear himself to his girlfriend's female relatives by helping out in the kitchen instead of hanging out with the men. The young man consciously subverts stereotypes in two key ways: First, by going against macho gender roles, he renders himself more attractive to the women ("a man who cooks!") while simultaneously demonstrating he is comfortable acknowledging his difference from the family. Second, he challenges the family's ethnic stereotype of him as an Other who is different from them when he responds in fluent Spanish to the mother's and grandmother's references to him as a handsome "Chino," Spanish for Chinese man. The end result of this kitchen episode is to highlight his suitability as a potential mate for their daughter, because he has established his command of the argot of the kitchen as well as of the family's mother tongue. As a DVD, the film's marketing department decided to blur the lines between viewing the film and mimicking its central plotline by including recipes for the dishes featured in the various households as a bonus "Special Feature."

Pieces of April, with its focus on multicultural cooking and interracial romance, showcases the difficulties people face in befriending one another in densely populated urban areas, like the New York City apartment where the events take place. Both of the other films took it as a given that people can forge and maintain emotional connections with others across barriers of class, language, and distance, but *Pieces of April* takes on the challenge of dramatizing the process through which one urban dweller can break through to another in a time of need. This was an important lesson that showed the influence of the 9/11 terrorist attacks.

The film depicts immigration alongside the phenomenon of internal dislocation whereby people whose families live in other states are drawn by the appeal of New York City and move there to try their luck. Rarely are these two parallel mobility narratives told in tandem. The eponymous protagonist, April Burns, is the prodigal daughter of a somewhat disapproving family from Pennsylvania, whose mother is dying from breast cancer. In a last-ditch effort to make amends, April invites her family to celebrate Thanksgiving at her tiny apartment, which she shares with her African American boyfriend and is located in a shady neighborhood. This marks a new twist on the "myth of return" narrative discussed earlier, where extended family members are expected to journey back to the household appointed as the metaphorical seat of the family. The family vacillates about whether or not to join April in her celebration, reading the location of her home as yet more proof of her failures. In a scene that could be compared to Gabriel's angry departure from the suburbs after his family starts eating turkey without him in *Avalon*, the Burns run back to their car without letting April know they have arrived and beat a hasty retreat to a nearby diner to strategize.

Meanwhile, inside, April is indeed living up to her family's low expectations. She only discovers her oven is broken once she is ready to cook the bird, and so the hapless young woman has to appeal to her neighbors for help. As Roger Ebert summarizes this suspense-building element in the film:

> The turkey is the problem. April's oven is broken, and that sends her on a quest through her building for someone with an oven she can borrow. Most of the neighbors are suspicious or hostile, but there's a Chinese family that illustrates the same message as "What's Cooking?": Thanksgiving is a reminder that all Americans, even Native Americans, are immigrants to this continent. (Ebert 2003)

Ebert's explicit allusion to the earlier film highlights their shared positive outlook toward Thanksgiving's power to make all Americans feel grateful for the diversity that characterizes their nation.

Like the Vietnamese family in *What's Cooking?*, the Burns decide that fast food, figured here as the offerings of a local diner, is preferable to trying to pretend to eat inedible turkey. Although the bird does not actually get charred, the Burns assume that April's lack of experience in the kitchen will put their health at risk. The events that ensue do not so much prove them wrong as they change the paradigm through which the food should be understood. In going door to door to appeal to neighbors for help with the various parts of her meal, April gains some useful kitchen tips and also realizes that her problems with her family are not as unique as she thought. As was the case in *What's Cooking?*, there is built-in diversity within April's building; among the neighbors who willingly let her into their homes are an African American couple and a Chinese extended family. Though none of the characters are Native American, April does voice their counternarrative of genocide and land dispossession when she unexpectedly finds herself explaining the history of the Thanksgiving tradition to her Chinese neighbors with the aid of a translator. She gives three different versions of the origin myth of this American holiday: the first is autobiographical, describing the Pilgrims as "people like me" who found their first year alone to be "really, really hard"; the second is a retelling of the story as genocide and Indian removal, a politically correct narrative that attests to her liberal education; and the third, which is the version that actually gets translated to the family, is when she finally settles upon the theme of interdependence as the reason for the holiday. The film then brings these various players together to celebrate in a communal Thanksgiving dinner, featuring turkey as the main dish and multiple side dishes contributed by each of the neighbors according to their own respective cultural traditions.

In *Pieces of April*, the substitute family of neighbors does indeed "cut the turkey without" waiting for April's real family, but the late-arriving Burns do not take the same offense to such a breach of etiquette as Gabriel did to the snub he suffered by his hungry, suburban Jewish clan in *Avalon*. As recent immigrants, the elder Krichinskys cannot take a chance with varying any aspect of the traditional Thanksgiving celebration, because to do so threatens their sense of security within their adopted country's social imaginary. The Burns, in contrast, are firmly ensconced within the dominant, white middle class, though their oldest daughter has struck out on her own, and thus can afford to be more flexible and enjoy the impromptu celebration without fear whatsoever that it would in any way impact their place in society.

Immigrants as Human-Interest News Stories during Thanksgiving

News writers seeking a break from the media coverage of impending Black Friday sales or the fanfare surrounding the presidential pardoning of the turkey often turn to immigrants to ask about their assimilation to the United States during this national holiday. Those immigrants who choose to respond to such interview requests often seize the occasion to convey their own patriotism through discussing the food that graces their table during the Thanksgiving meal. Others convey their own sense of American-ness literally, by opening their doors to those newly arrived to the country and introducing them to one of our most distinctive culinary traditions: the serving of the roast turkey. These human-interest stories are aimed at a wide reading public, but they have a special appeal to readers of the memoir-with-recipe genre because of the central role of the life story told through the lens of food, and often accompanied by either a photo of the immigrant, or else a recipe for his or her take on the staples of the Thanksgiving meal. The news interviews with immigrants described below exemplify or touch upon some of the themes discussed in connection with the Thanksgiving films, thereby adding a bit of realism to the cinematic depictions of immigrant family celebrations.

The first theme that emerges from the holiday news features is a discussion of how the turkey should be prepared. As was the case in the Vietnamese household depicted in *What's Cooking?*, opinion is split as to whether the turkey should be seasoned only with salt and pepper in the manner generally held to be "traditional," or whether one's preferred seasonings (olive oil, garlic, onions) or cooking techniques (boiling and stewing the turkey pieces, serving just a breast) will have the day. In a 2004 article in the *New York Times*, reporter Kim Severson finds that those who choose a "traditional" preparation often face what she calls "the most American of problems": dry breast meat on the roasted bird. The perception that the roast turkey is compulsory runs deep with some naturalized citizens, as evidenced by the comments made by a Palestinian immigrant from Paterson, New Jersey, who had spent more than twenty years living in the United States. Severson quotes him as saying, "I live in America. You tell me to eat turkey, I'm going to eat turkey" (Severson 2004). This particular comment simultaneously implies that immigrants like him have no personal freedom when it comes to deciding whether to choose to celebrate Thanksgiving or not since it is somehow held to be the law of the land, so to speak; it also shows the speaker's lingering reluctance to identify himself as an "American" or even a naturalized citizen. The closest he gets to this is by pointing to his place of residence as the reason why he will comply with the behavior expected of other Americans.

The second theme that emerges from Thanksgiving stories is that of determining levels of assimilation to mainstream U.S. culture by weighing the relative authenticity of the menu served during the holiday meal. American-born children of immigrants are sometimes so culturally integrated into their families' culinary heritage that it takes them a while to catch on to the fact that their domestic versions of Thanksgiving meals would not pass muster as "traditional." Interviewing immigrants about their holiday meals for a story in the "Communities" forum of the *Washington Times.com*, April Thompson found someone whose memories of childhood celebrations met such a pattern:

> Erika Franz's father was born in Yugoslavia and spent his teen and early adult years in Germany after World War II. The differences in her family's Thanksgivings were subtle: sauce instead of gravy, occasionally an Austrian torte rather than pie, and not always turkey but another type of fowl. "I was scandalized when I was old enough to realize, first that my folks bought a turkey breast instead of a whole turkey, then again when my folks switched to Cornish game hens," Franz said. Although, this disapproval changed as she got older. "I went from offended that my parents were being different to proud that we did it differently." (Thompson 2013)

Unlike the previous passage, where teenagers convey their views that there is only one correct protein with which to celebrate the Thanksgiving holiday, Thompson's interlocutor undergoes an evolution in her understanding and appreciation of her family's unique spin on Thanksgiving. By consciously deviating from both American and Yugoslavian/German canonical foods in their choices, the Franz family demonstrates yet another attitude traditionally associated with the American national character: individualism. Thompson concludes that as long as immigrants keep coming to America, "no doubt we'll adopt foods and traditions from their home countries" (Thompson 2013). That trend has already started, with children beginning to learn about celebrations from other cultural traditions at school and states around the country hosting their own Cinco de Mayo and Chinese New Year's celebrations, even if the attendant menus are still in flux.

The promotion of assimilation was indeed the reason why public school teachers during the Progressive Era (1900–1920) seized upon this secular holiday as a means of trying to ease their immigrant students' integration into American society. As she traces the evolution of public Thanksgiving observances into the domestic celebration that it has become today, historian Elizabeth Pleck points to schools as the social institutions with the biggest opportunity to carry out the nationalizing project of promoting a common American culture:

> The schools recognized that they had to develop an emotional bond between the immigrant and the nation, a love of country. Immigrant children could be taught American history and learn about the holidays, but the home was where the deepest feelings of patriotism were conveyed. Thus, the home celebration of holidays needed to be encouraged to reinforce the patriotism learned in the school. By holding a feast around a common table, an immigrant family could demonstrate its acceptance of American customs and knowledge of American history. (Pleck 2001, 780)

This desire to use the curriculum to effect both children's and their parents' acculturation culminated in the invention of the school Thanksgiving pageant, a tradition whereby school children were divided into Pilgrims and Indians, made their own costumes, and invited their parents to watch them stage a reenactment of the first Thanksgiving meal shared between these two groups. Teachers prepared their students beforehand by reading stories about this "first meal," presenting the occasion as a foundational myth of origin, and seizing upon the importance of shared family meals as a national value.

Severson's article also confirms that schools still serve as the primary cultural gateway through which immigrants with children first learn about the holiday and its iconic meal: "the finer points of the holiday are often lost on many immigrant parents, who are often introduced to Thanksgiving when their children come home with recipe cards and construction-paper turkeys" (Severson 2004). As the experience of one of the people whom she interviewed can attest, these same children are often the most ardent examples of "culinary policing," loudly voicing their objections if their parents' feast does not resemble the one they learned about in school. Four years later, Melanie Kirkpatrick interviewed a group of teenagers attending Newcomer School in New York City, an institution directly geared toward immigrant children, and asked them whether they thought it necessary to prepare the turkey for the Thanksgiving meal. The teens seemed incredulous that someone would question the bird's symbolic value:

> The kids all seem familiar with Thanksgiving's food traditions and more than half of those I speak to say they plan to celebrate at home with the festive bird. There are nontraditional foods on the menu, too. A Polish girl mentions pierogies. A Chinese boy says his family will eat rice. When I ask whether it really matters what you eat on Thanksgiving, I get a bunch of "you've gotta be kidding" looks. "Yes, it's tradition!" shouts one student.

"Remember the history of the country," admonishes another. (Kirkpatrick 2008)

Kirkpatrick takes it as a good sign that immigrant children are well acquainted with American history and cultural traditions, but it is a bit difficult not to read this exchange as a bit of a citizenship test. For example, her use of "nontraditional" as an adjective to describe the side dishes that the students' transnational families will be serving gives normative power to what I have been calling "canonical foods" (turkey, mashed potatoes, cranberry sauce, and sweet potatoes), at the expense of foods that are indeed "traditional" to the immigrants' own foodways, like the pierogies or rice instead of potatoes. Whereas the *Wall Street Journal* reporter could tolerate variations as long as they are not confused with the "real thing," Thompson's general attitude toward the culinary modifications the immigrants she interviewed have made to the canonical holiday menu is a lot more welcoming than was Kirkpatrick's.

The normativity of the Thanksgiving menu was codified most clearly by Norman Rockwell's iconic 1943 Thanksgiving cover for the *Saturday Evening Post*, a painting called "Freedom from Want." The roasted turkey takes center stage, flanked by the eager and expectant (white) faces of a family assembled at the table, eager to begin the feast. This idealized image, produced in wartime, contains all of the culinary elements that have come to have canonical status at a Thanksgiving celebration: roasted turkey, sweet potatoes, molded cranberry sauce, and mashed potatoes. Thus, it models not only the behavior (assembling together to eat a family meal) but also the menu of an all-American holiday spread.

Though this image is homogeneous in its depiction of Thanksgiving as a family ritual, not all publicly disseminated images related to the holiday have promoted Euro-American whiteness as the default norm of mainstream society in the United Sates. Sociologist Amy Adamcyzk references another influential popular depiction of the Thanksgiving feast dating back to the nineteenth century: Thomas Nast's political cartoon for *Harper's*, depicting "Uncle Sam's Thanksgiving Dinner" (1869). In her article tracing the development of Thanksgiving celebrations, Adamczyk explains the ideology embedded within the scene the cartoon depicts:

> [It] shows an optimistic view of the holiday as a metaphor for peaceful diversity of the nation. Beneath the portraits of Lincoln, Washington, and President Grant, Uncle Sam carves a turkey for his multinational guests,

which include Columbia (The United States) seated between an Asian family that is being hosted by an African-American family. Included in the scene are mottoes like "Come One, Come All," "Free and Equal," "Self-Government," and "Universal Suffrage." (Adamczyk 2002, 350–51)

The date of the political cartoon is important—it is four years after the end of the Civil War, while Reconstruction and carpetbagging were reshaping the former Confederacy into a New South, but also a mere ten years since the xenophobic nativism of the Know-Nothing party was a force to contend against in the national political landscape. The Chinese Exclusion Act would not be passed until 1882, so this was a brief window of time where the thought of a peaceful coexistence of multiple races around one common holiday table could be entertained in the afterglow of Emancipation. Though she acknowledges that such optimism was far from the prevailing view of race relations and immigration at the time, Adamczyk nonetheless takes comfort in such an imagined or projected image of racial unity.

Today's Hollywood films and newspaper human-interest features perform the same function. They depict an idealized version of an open and accepting American society, where immigrants feel welcome to participate in rituals of national belonging, like Thanksgiving celebrations, while also sharing details about their domestic lives with their interested compatriots. What they affirm, however, is not the specific menu or the accuracy of the holiday's historical framework, but the value of people coming together to negotiate tradition and ritual to form new and reinvigorate existing families and communities. Each of these texts is framed in such a way as to maintain the immigrants' dignity, even as they satisfy the U.S.-born audience's curiosity about the other: the films are packaged as entertainment, and the interviews are a seasonally appropriate way to render the yearly observance of Thanksgiving "newsworthy" by portraying its charms anew through the "fresh eyes" of recent arrivals. What the memoirs with recipes make clear, though, is that immigrants would like to take control of these "normalizing" narratives that preach culinary assimilation as the key to successful integration into mainstream American culture. The picture they paint of their lives as naturalized citizens and their descendants are more complex—spicier, even—than the "vanilla" versions promulgated through mass media and popular culture. Finding one's way in a new country is a daunting challenge, and one that does not involve a wholesale reinvention of the person to fit the new circumstances. The emotional effects of this geographical rupture take decades, even generations, to fully work themselves out. A little comfort food makes letting go of the old, and developing a taste for the new, a bit less disorienting. By inviting the reader into their personal lives to learn more about how fraught some food choices can be and also sharing some of their favorite recipes, immigrant writers and those who are descended from immigrants show their hospitality and dedication to keeping a place at the table ready to welcome strangers.

Works Cited

Abu-Jaber, Diana. *The Language of Baklava: A Memoir*. New York: Pantheon Books, 2005. Print.

Adamczyk, Amy. "On Thanksgiving and Collective Memory: Constructing the American Tradition." *Journal of Historical Sociology* 15.3 (2002): 343–65. Print.

Anderson, Benedict. *Imagined Communities: Reflections on the Origin and Spread of Nationalism (New Edition)*. New York: Verso, 2006. Print.

Angelou, Maya. *Hallelujah! The Welcome Table: A Lifetime of Memories With Recipes*. New York: Random House, 2004. Print.

Avalon. Dir. Barry Levinson. Tri-Star Pictures, 1990. Film.

Barthes, Roland. "Reading Brillat Savarin." *The Rustle of Language*. Trans. Richard Howard. Berkeley: University of California Press, 1989. 250–70. Print.

Beard, James. *Delights and Prejudices*. 1964. Philadelphia, PA: Running Press, 2001. Print.

Bhimji, Fazila. "Cosmopolitan Belonging and Diaspora: Second-Generation British Muslim Women Travelling to South Asia." *Citizenship Studies* 12.4 (2008): 413–27. Print.

Bittman, Mark. "Rethinking the Word 'Foodie.'" *New York Times*. 22 June 2014. Web. 3 May 2015.

Boyarin, Daniel, and Jonathan Boyarin. "Diaspora: Generation and the Ground of Jewish Identity." *Critical Inquiry* (1993): 693–725. Print.

Buchanan, Angela B., Nora G. Albert, and Daniel Beaulieu. "The Population with Haitian Ancestry in the United States: 2009." United States Census Bureau. October 2010. Print.

Carballo, Viviana. *Havana Salsa: Stories and Recipes*. New York: Atria Books, 2006. Print.

Chávez, Denise. *A Taco Testimony: Meditations on Family, Food and Culture*. Tucson, AZ: Rio Nuevo Publishers, 2006. Print.

Clarke, Austin. *Pig Tails 'n Breadfruit: A Culinary Memoir*. New York: The New Press, 1999. Print.

Clifford, James. *Routes: Travel and Translation in the Late Twentieth Century*. Cambridge, MA: Harvard University Press, 1997. Print.

Conde, Yvonne M. *Operation Pedro Pan: The Untold Exodus of 14,000 Children*. London: Taylor & Francis, 2000. Print.

Copage, Eric V. *Kwanzaa: An African-American Celebration of Culture and Cooking*. New York: William Morrow & Company, 1991. Print.

Cox, John L. "The Overseas Student: Expatriate, Sojourner or Settler?" *Acta Psychiatrica Scandinavica* 78.S344 (1988): 179–84. Print.

DeSalvo, Louise. *Crazy in the Kitchen: Food, Feuds, and Forgiveness in an Italian American Family*. New York: Bloomsbury, 2004. Print.

Diner, Hasia R. *Hungering for America: Italian, Irish, Foodways in the Age of Migration*. Cambridge, MA: Harvard University Press, 2001. Print.

Du Bois, W. E. B. *The Souls of Black Folk*. 1903. Ed. Henry Louis Gates Jr. and Terri Hume Oliver. New York: W. W. Norton & Company, 1999. Print.

Ebert, Roger. "Pieces of April." *RogerEbert.com*. 24 October 2003. Web. 3 December 2013.

———. "What's Cooking?" *RogerEbert.com*. 17 November 2000. Web. 3 December 2013.

Edge, John T., Elizabeth Engelhardt, and Ted Ownby, eds. *The Larder: Food Studies Methods from the American South*. Athens: The University of Georgia Press, 2013. Print.

Ehrlich, Elizabeth. *Miriam's Kitchen: A Memoir*. New York: Penguin, 1997. Print.

Engelhardt, Elizabeth. "Redrawing the Grocery: Practices and Methods for Studying Southern Food." Edge, Engelhardt, and Ownby 1–6. Print.

Foer, Jonathan Safran. *Eating Animals*. New York: Little, Brown & Company, 2009. Print.

———, ed. *New American Haggadah*. Trans. Nathan Englander. New York: Little, Brown & Company, 2012a. Print.

———. "Why a Haggadah?" *New York Times*. 1 April 2012b. Web. 18 November 2013.

Furiya, Linda. *Bento Box in the Heartland: My Japanese Girlhood in Whitebread America*. Berkeley, CA: Seal Press, 2006. Print.

———. *How to Cook a Dragon: Living, Loving, and Eating in China*. Berkeley, CA: Seal Press, 2008. Print.

Gabaccia, Donna. *We Are What We Eat: Ethnic Food and the Making of Americans*. Cambridge, MA: Harvard University Press, 1998. Print.

Green, Nancy L. "Expatriation, Expatriates, and Expats: The American Transformation of a Concept." *The American Historical Review* 114.2 (2009): 307–28. Print.

Gregory, James N. *The Southern Diaspora: How the Great Migrations of Black and White Southerners Transformed America*. Chapel Hill: The University of North Carolina Press, 2005. Kindle edition.

Goldman, Anne E. *Take My Word: Autobiographical Innovations of Ethnic American Working Women*. Berkeley: University of California Press, 1996. Print.

Heldke, Lisa. *Exotic Appetites: Ruminations of a Food Adventurer*. New York: Routledge, 2005. Print.

Hirsch, Marianne. *The Generation of Postmemory: Writing and Visual Culture after the Holocaust.* New York: Columbia University Press, 2012. Kindle edition.

Hobsbawm, Eric, and Terence Ranger, eds. *The Invention of Tradition.* 1983. Croydon: Cambridge University Press, 2013. Print.

Hoggart, Richard. *The Uses of Literacy.* 1957. New Brunswick, NJ: Transaction Publishers, 2008. Print.

Hutcheon, Linda. "A Crypto-Ethnic Confession." *The Anthology of Italian-Canadian Writing.* Ed. Joseph Pivato. Vol. 52. Toronto: Guernica Editions, 1998. 314–23. Kindle edition.

Jaffrey, Madhur. *Climbing the Mango Trees: A Memoir of a Childhood in India.* New York: Alfred A. Knopf, 2007. Print.

———. *An Invitation to Indian Cooking.* New York: Vintage, 1973. Kindle edition.

Joseph, Betty. "Cultural Forms and World Systems: The Ethnic Epic in the New Diaspora." *New Routes for Diaspora Studies.* Ed. Sukanya Banerjee, Aims McGuinness, and Steven C. McKay. Bloomington: Indiana University Press, 2012. 208–28. Print.

Kennedy, John F. *A Nation of Immigrants.* 1964. New York: HarperCollins, 2008. Print.

Kirkpatrick, Melanie. "Cross Country: What Newcomers Know About Thanksgiving." *The Wall Street Journal.* 29 November 2008. Web. 6 December 2013.

Kulp, Joshua. "The Origins of the Seder and Haggadah." *Currents in Biblical Research* 4.1 (2005): 109–34. Print.

Lee, Edward. *Smoke and Pickles: Recipes and Stories from a New Southern Kitchen.* New York: Artisan, 2013. Print.

Li, Leslie. *Daughter of Heaven: A Memoir with Earthly Recipes.* New York: Arcade Publishing, 2005. Print.

Lin-Liu, Jen. *On the Noodle Road: From Beijing to Rome with Love and Pasta.* New York: Riverhead Books, 2013. Print.

———. *Serve the People: A Stir-fried Journey through China.* Orlando, FL: Harcourt, 2008. Print.

Liu, Eric. "Asian or American?: John Huang, Dual Loyalty and the Myth of Dual Identity." *Slate.com.* 15 November 1996. Web. 11 June 2015.

Louie, Andrea. "When You Are Related to the 'Other': (Re)locating the Chinese Mainland in Asian American Politics Through Cultural Tourism." *Positions* 11.3 (2003): 735–65. Print.

Lowe, Lisa. *Immigrant Acts: On Asian American Cultural Politics.* Durham, NC: Duke University Press, 1996. Print.

Machado, Eduardo, and Michael Domitrovich. *Tastes Like Cuba: An Exile's Hunger for Home.* New York: Gotham Books, 2007. Print.

Mannur, Anita. *Culinary Fictions: Food in South Asian Diasporic Culture.* Philadelphia: Temple University Press, 2009. Print.

Morris, Christopher. *Becoming Southern: The Evolution of a Way of Life, Warren County and Vicksburg, Mississippi, 1770–1860.* New York: Oxford University Press, 1995. Print.

Muhlke, Christine. "Heartburn." *New York Times* Sunday Book Review. 29 May 2009. Web. 12 December 2013.

Nance, Susan. "Respectability and Representation: The Moorish Science Temple, Morocco, and Black Public Culture in 1920s Chicago." *American Quarterly* 54.4 (2002): 623–59. Print.

Nguyen, Bich Mihn. *Stealing Buddha's Dinner: A Memoir.* New York: Viking Adult, 2007. Print.

O'Keefe, Dan. *The Real Festivus: The True Story Behind America's Favorite Made-Up Holiday.* New York: Perigee Book, 2005. Print.

Oyangen, Knut. "The Gastrodynamics of Displacement: Place-Making and Gustatory Identity in the Immigrants' Midwest." *Journal of Interdisciplinary History* 39.3 (2009): 323–48. Print.

Palmié, Stephan. "Intangible Cultural Property, Semiotic Ideology, and the Vagrancies of Ethnoculinary Recognition." *African Arts* 42.4 (2009): 54–61. Print.

Perralton, Hilary. *Learning Abroad: A History of the Commonwealth Scholarship and Fellowship Plan.* Cambridge: Cambridge Scholars Publishing, 2009. Print.

Pieces of April. Dir. Peter Hedges. MGM, 2003. Film.

Pinner, Patty. *Sweets: Soul Food Desserts & Memories.* 2003. Berkeley, CA: Ten Speed Press, 2006. Print.

Pleck, Elizabeth. "Kwanzaa and the Black Nationalist Tradition, 1966–1990." *Journal of American Ethnic History* 20.4 (2001): 3–28. Print.

———. "The Making of the Domestic Occasion: The History of Thanksgiving in the United States." *Journal of Social History* (1999): 773–89. Print.

Probyn, Elspeth. *Carnal Appetites: FoodSexIdentities.* New York: Routledge, 2000. Print.

Ramsdell, Kristin. *Romance Fiction: A Guide to the Genre.* Westport, CT: Libraries Unlimited, 1999. Print.

Randelman, Mary Urrutia, and Joan Schwartz. *Memories of a Cuban Kitchen.* New York: Wiley Publishing, 1992. Print.

Ray, Krishnendu. *The Migrant's Table: Meals and Memories in Bengali-American Households.* Philadelphia: Temple University Press, 2004. Print.

"Recipes." United States Copyright Office. 06 February 2012. Web. 7 July 2014.

Rockwell, Norman. "Freedom from Want." *Saturday Evening Post* 6 (1943). Print.

Rossant, Colette. *Apricots on the Nile: A Memoir with Recipes.* New York: Washington Square Press, 2004a. Print.

———. *Return to Paris.* New York: Washington Square Press, 2004b. Print.

———. *The World in My Kitchen: The Adventures of a (Mostly) French Woman in America.* New York: Atria, 2006. Print.

Schultermandl, Silvia. *Transnational Matrilineage: Mother-Daughter Conflict in Asian American Literature.* Berlin: LIT Verlag Münster, 2009. Print.

Severson, Kim. "Turkey Is Basic, But Immigrants Add Their Homeland Touches." *The New York Times.* 25 November 2004. Web. 6 December 2013.

Shange, Ntzoake. *If I Can Cook / You Know God Can.* Boston: Beacon Press, 1998. Print.

———. *Sassafrass, Cypress and Indigo: A Novel.* 1982. New York: Picador, 1996. Print.

Smith, Sidonie, and Julia Watson. *Reading Autobiography: Interpreting Life Narratives.* Minneapolis: University of Minnesota Press, 2010. Print.

Southern Foodways Alliance. "About Us." *Southern Foodways Alliance.* n.d. Web. 8 June 2015.

Sunée, Kim. *Trail of Crumbs: Hunger, Love, and the Search for Home.* New York: Grand Central Publishing, 2008. Print.

Tan, Cheryl Lu-Lien. *A Tiger in the Kitchen: A Memoir of Food and Family.* New York: Hyperion, 2011. Print.

Thompson, April. "Immigrants Enjoy and Enhance Thanksgiving Celebrations." *The Washington Times.com.* 28 November 2013. Web. 6 December 2013.

Triay, Victor Andrés. *Fleeing Castro: Operation Pedro Pan and the Children's Program.* Gainesville, FL: University Press of Florida, 1999. Print.

Vargas-Ramos, Carlos, and Juan C. García-Ellín. "Demographic Transitions: Settlement and Distribution of Puerto Rican Populations in the United States." Center for Puerto Rican Studies Research Brief. Hunter College, NY. July 2013. 1–4. Print.

Von Bremzen, Anya. *Mastering the Art of Soviet Cooking: A Memoir of Food and Longing.* New York: Random House Digital, 2013. Print.

Von Bremzen, Anya, and John C. Welchman. *Please to the Table: The Russian Cookbook.* New York: Workman Publishing, 1990. Print.

Warnes, Andrew. "Edgeland Terroir: Authenticity and Invention inNew Southern Foodways Strategy." Edge, Engelhardt, and Ownby 345–362. Print.

What's Cooking? Dir. Gurinder Chadha. Because Entertainment, Flashpoint, 2000. Film.

Williams-Forson, Psyche A. *Building Houses Out of Chicken Legs: Black Women, Food, and Power.* Chapel Hill: University of North Carolina Press, 2006. Print.

Witt, Doris. *Black Hunger: Soul Food and America.* Minneapolis: University of Minnesota Press, 2004. Print.

Zangwill, Israel. *The Melting Pot: Drama in Four Acts.* 1909. New York: Macmillan, 1910. Print.

Further Reading

Baena, Rosilía. "Gastro-graphy: Food as Metaphor in Fred Wah's *Diamond Grill* and Austin Clarke's *Pig Tails 'n Breadfruit.*" *Canadian Ethnic Studies* 38.1 (2006): 105. Print.

Geist, Edward. "Cooking Bolshevik: Anastas Mikoian and the Making of the Book about Delicious and Healthy Food." *The Russian Review* 71.2 (2012): 295–313. Print.

Gilbert, Elizabeth. *Eat, Pray, Love: One Woman's Search for Everything Across Italy, India and Indonesia.* New York: Penguin, 2007. Print.

Hirsch, Marianne. "Projected Memory: Holocaust Photographs in Personal and Public Fantasy." *Acts of Memory: Cultural Recall in the Present.* Ed. Mieke Bal, Jonathan Crewe, and Leo Spitzer. Hanover, NH: University Press of New England, 1999. 3–23. Print.

Mannur, Anita. "Culinary Nostalgia: Authenticity, Nationalism and Diaspora." *MELUS* 32.4 (2007): 12. Print.

Narayan, Shoba. *Monsoon Diary: A Memoir with Recipes*. New York: Random House Trade Paperbacks, 2004. Print.

Portes, Alejandro. "Introduction: Immigration and Its Aftermath." *International Migration Review* (1994): 632–39. Print.

Rombauer, Irma S., and Marion Rombauer Becker. *Joy of Cooking*. Indianapolis, IN: The Bobbs-Merrill Company, 1967. Print.

Roy, Parama. *Alimentary Tracts: Appetites, Aversions, and the Postcolonial*. Durham, NC: Duke University Press, 2010. Print.

Schechner, Richard. *Performance Studies: An Introduction*. 2nd ed. New York: Routledge/Taylor & Francis Group, 2002. Print.

Sollors, Werner. *Beyond Ethnicity: Consent and Descent in American Culture*. New York: Oxford University Press, 1986. Print.

———, ed. *The Invention of Ethnicity*. New York: Oxford University Press, 1989. Print.

U.S. Department of Justice. "Adjustment of Status under the 1966 Cuban Refugee Adjustment Act." Web.

Index

Abu-Jaber, Diana, 4, 6–7, 9, 13–14, 16, 42–43, 45–46, 48–51, 53–56, 59–62
academic sojourner, 15, 21–23, 30, 35
acculturation, 2n1, 3n2, 4, 13, 20, 50, 90, 100, 108, 138
American-ness, 6, 51n1, 56, 65, 89, 91, 96, 106, 136
Angelou, Maya, 4, 13–14, 17, 66–67, 69–71, 76, 78, 86
Apricots on the Nile (Rossant), 16, 42, 50, 56, 58n3, 62
Assimilation, 3n2, 4, 7, 13–14, 16, 20, 39, 42, 44–45, 48, 51, 93, 109, 111, 117, 128–29, 131, 133, 136–37, 140
Avalon, 20, 128–31, 134–35

Beard, James, 12, 14
Becoming Southern (Morris), 17, 67
Bento Box in the Heartland (Furiya), 16, 42, 47, 52, 56, 62

Carballo, Viviana, 9, 17, 66–67, 74–75, 77–80, 86
Chavez, Denise, 4, 13–14, 17, 66–67, 74–75, 77–80, 86
citizens, 4, 7–8, 20, 42, 81n10, 93, 108, 136, 140; citizenship, 1–2n1, 9–10, 21, 44–45, 62, 82, 91, 93–95, 102, 138; culinary citizenship, 10, 35, 42, 44, 69, 75, 78, 82, 85

Clarke, Austin, ix, 4, 13–16, 21–24, 26–37, 39
Climbing the Mango Trees (Jaffrey), 15, 21, 23–24, 30–31, 39
compatriots, 7, 39, 42, 95, 107, 140
Copage, Eric V., 19, 110, 121–23, 125
coupled-self, 89, 98–99, 101, 107
crypto foreigner, 6–7, 91, 95–96
culinary Americanization, 44–46, 48–49
culinary policing, 129, 132–33, 138
cultural translator, 28, 43, 78, 81
culture shock, 2n1, 5, 90

Daughter of Heaven (Li), 16, 42, 56, 60–62
diaspora, 10, 16–17, 19, 32, 37, 55, 60, 62, 66, 68–69, 71, 73–75, 79, 81n10, 82, 104, 110–12, 112n1, 116, 118–19, 121, 126
displacement, 4, 7, 17, 22, 66, 68n2, 76, 101, 111
diversity, 6, 8, 17, 51, 78, 116, 134–35, 139

eating subjects, 14, 79
Ehrlich, Elizabeth, 19, 110, 114–17
exile, 9, 17, 20, 60, 66, 68–69, 75–81
expatriate(s), 18, 88–95, 97–98, 103, 105–6, 108, 110; expatriation 4, 6, 89, 92–93, 108

Foer, Jonathan Safran, 19, 110, 116–17, 121
food adventurers, 18, 89–90

149

150 * Index

foodies, 5, 77, 107
foodscape, 10, 39, 78
Furiya, Linda, 9, 16, 18, 42–43, 45–53, 55–58, 62, 88–92, 94–96, 100n1, 102–8

Gabaccia, Donna R., 10, 39n3, 44
gasrographic revisionism, 19, 112–13, 123, 125
gastronomic surveillance, 41, 45–50, 62, 129
Great Migration, 4, 17, 68, 71
Gregory, James N., 17, 68

half-immigrant, v, 2–5, 7–8, 14, 42, 45–46, 50–51, 53, 55–56 59, 62, 130
Hallelujah! The Welcome Table (Angelou), 17, 66, 69, 70, 86
Hart-Cellar Act, 9
Havana Salsa (Carballo), 17, 66, 75, 77–80, 86
Heldke, Lisa, 18, 89, 90
heritage tourism, 41–42, 55, 58, 61–62
Hobsbawm, Eric, 19, 109, 111, 113, 119
Hoggart, Richard, 15, 22, 24–27
homeland, 7, 11, 15–16, 22, 30, 35, 39, 41–42, 55–56, 60, 62, 78, 92–93, 96, 109–10, 112
homesick, 3, 69; homesickness, 60, 68, 77
How to Cook a Dragon (Furiya), 18, 88–89, 91–94, 96, 100n1, 102–3, 105, 108

If I Can Cook / You Know God Can (Shange), 19, 110, 118–19, 125
imagined community, 4, 6–7, 68, 90, 102, 108, 116, 123
immigrant, 2–10, 12, 14–17, 20–21, 28, 34, 37, 39–46, 48–49, 51–58, 60–62, 64, 66, 68n2, 74, 76, 87–88, 90, 93, 96, 106, 108–10, 114, 116–17, 120, 125, 127–30, 134–141
immigration, 2n1, 4–10, 13–14, 17, 20, 35, 37, 42–43, 52–54, 62, 68n2, 76, 90, 93, 96, 108, 125, 127, 129, 131, 134, 140
invented traditions, 6, 19, 109, 110, 112, 114, 117–18, 121, 124, 127

Jaffrey, Madhur, 4, 13–15, 21–24, 26–27, 30–34, 36–39, 77

Kwanzaa (Copage), 19, 110, 121, 123, 125

The Language of Baklava (Abu-Jaber), 6, 16, 42, 48, 56, 60–62

Lee, Edward, 14, 64–66
Li, Leslie, 9, 16, 42–43, 45–56, 60–62
Lin-Liu, Jen, 18, 89–92, 94–96, 105–8

Machado, Eduardo, 4, 13–14, 17, 66–67, 74, 79–83
Manifest Destiny, 17, 68
Mannur, Anita, 10, 30n, 44
Mastering the Art of Soviet Cooking (Von Bremzen), 19–20, 110, 124–25
McCarran-Walter Act, 8–9
memoir with recipes, x, 4–8, 10, 12–14, 16, 19, 22, 27, 30, 37, 42, 57, 67–68, 78n7, 86, 90, 94, 96–97, 99, 101, 105, 108, 110, 113, 124, 127, 129, 136, 140
Memories of a Cuban Kitchen (Randelman), 17, 66, 75, 79, 86
Miriam's Kitchen (Ehrlich), 19, 110, 114, 116, 125
myth of return, 129, 131, 134

nativism, 8, 117, 140
naturalized citizens, 4, 7, 42, 93, 108, 136, 140
New American Haggadah (Foer), 19, 110, 116–17, 121, 123, 125
Nostalgia, 7, 34, 43, 62, 65, 67, 68n2, 69n3, 78–79, 109

O'Keefe, Daniel, 19, 110, 123–24, 126–27
On the Noodle Road (Lin-Liu), 18, 88–89, 91–93, 95, 105, 107–8

Pedro Pan, 74, 79n8
Pieces of April, 20, 128–29, 131, 133, 135
Pig Tails 'n Breadfruit (Clarke), ix, 15, 21, 23–24, 27–29, 35, 37, 39
Pinner, Patty, 17, 66–67, 71–74, 76

Ray, Krishnendu, 14, 23, 34
The Real Festivus (O'Keefe), 19, 110, 123
Refugees, 9, 78, 79n8
respectable exoticism, 22–23, 30, 34, 48
Return to Paris (Rossant), 16, 42, 50, 56, 58n, 62
Rossant, Colette, 4, 14, 16, 18, 42–43, 50–51, 54, 56–59, 62, 88–92, 94, 96–99, 105, 108

scholarship boy, 15, 21–22, 24–27, 31, 33, 35, 38, 41
scholarship girl, 22, 30–31, 33, 38, 41

Serve the People (Lin-Liu), 18, 88–89, 91–93, 95, 105, 107–8
settler migrants, 15, 21–24, 34–35
Shange, Ntozake, 4, 13–14, 19, 110, 118–20, 122, 125
Slavery, 17, 68, 76, 118, 122, 125
Smoke and Pickles (Lee), 17, 64
The Southern Diaspora (Gregory), 17, 68
Sunée, Kim, 18, 88–92, 94–96, 99–102, 106–8
Sweets (Pinner), 17, 66, 71–72, 86

A Taco Testimony (Chavez), 17, 66, 82–83, 86
Tan, Cheryl Lu-Lien, 15, 21–27, 32–34, 37–39, 77
taste memory (beard), 12, 30, 34
Tastes Like Cuba (Machado), 17, 66, 79, 80, 81n10, 82, 85–86

Thanksgiving, xi, 1, 3, 6, 20, 128–130, 134–40
A Tiger in the Kitchen (Tan), 15, 21, 23–24, 33, 37–38, 40
Trail of Crumbs (Sunee), 18, 88–89, 91–93, 101–2, 105, 108
transnational matrilineage, 60–61
transnational networks, 20, 33, 39, 102

Urrutia Randelman, Mary, 9, 17, 66–67, 74–76, 79–80, 86

Von Bremzen, Anya, 19, 110, 124–27

What's Cooking?, 20, 128–29, 131, 134–36
The World in My Kitchen (Rossant), 18, 89, 91–93, 95, 105, 108

www.ingramcontent.com/pod-product-compliance
Lightning Source LLC
Chambersburg PA
CBHW030140240426
43672CB00005B/200